W9-COI-940

LIFE of the
PARTY

LIFE of the PARTY

STORIES OF A PERPETUAL MAN-CHILD

BERT KREISCHER

ST. MARTIN'S PRESS ❧ NEW YORK

www.stmartins.com

Designed by Steven Seighman

The Library of Congress Cataloging-in-Publication Data is available
upon request.

ISBN 978-1-250-03025-2 (hardcover)
ISBN 978-1-250-03031-3 (e-book)

St. Martin's Press books may be purchased for educational, business, or
promotional use. For information on bulk purchases, please contact
Macmillan Corporate and Premium Sales Department at 1-800-221-7945,
extension 5442, or write specialmarkets@macmillan.com.

First Edition: June 2014

10 9 8 7 6 5 4 3 2 1

CONTENTS

ACKNOWLEDGMENTS

In fear of forgetting to thank someone important for the help in making this book possible, I would like to simply thank my family.

Dad, you footed the bill for a lot of these stories, so you may not want to read past this page. In all seriousness, you have always told me to write a book, and here it is. Thank you for making me the man I am today. You'll never know how important that one phone call on my twenty-sixth birthday was.

Mom, you have been my champion since I was a little boy. You have had my back since that first fly ball I caught, spiked, and started dancing in the infield. As the coaches screamed, the bases cleared, and Denny Sullivan yelled, "Put some mustard on that hot dog," you cheered in the stands for me. I can't imagine who I'd be without your love and support.

To my sisters, Annie and Kottie, you didn't really do much to help me write this book, shape me, or support me. This book would be just as good had you done nothing, which you kind of did. Really, you two have just been there, like two gas stations you pass by every day on your way to work. Maybe I'll stop and get a coffee, maybe a donut, some gas, whatever . . . just kidding. I love you like sisters, BIG TEAM!

To my daughters, Georgia and Ila, I love you SO much more than my sisters. You guys gave me purpose, direction, and a reason to slow down. Ironically, you are also the reasons I work so hard. Considering you guys are only seven and nine right now, I'll keep it simple. Realize, if and when you read this book, that your dad is ALSO the guy who taught you to ride your bikes, played monkey in the middle with you, and kissed you four times every night I tucked you into bed. Nailed it! Oh it is on! My only hope is that this book is out of print by the time you go to college.

LeeAnn, you are simply the greatest person to ever come into my life. You are not only the reason this book is complete, you are the reason that I am complete. I wake up every day the happiest man in the world, thanking God I have you in my life. Thank you for your absolute selflessness day in and day out. I only hope that one day the roles can be reversed and I can be as selfless for you as you have been for me. I love you, baby doll!

LIFE of the PARTY

Introduction

Bong hits are like strippers: they're best when shared with a group of friends. That's what I was doing—taking a bong hit among friends—when I got the phone call that would change my life. There have been a handful of times when I knew without a doubt that my life was now changing. All of them are in this book, and none of them would have happened if it weren't for this one phone call.

"It's *Rolling Stone* magazine," my roommate Blair said, passing me the phone. "They asked for you." Had I known what was coming, I might have paid more attention, but I was a sixth-year senior with no plans beyond that toke and my next game of Frisbee golf. So instead, I held in the smoke and bubbled out a hello. As best I can recall, the man on the other end explained that he was a journalist and was interested in writing an article on my college, Florida State University, being "The Number One Party School in the Country." He needed a tour guide, he said, who knew the school inside and out. Since my name had been brought up by nearly everyone he had spoken with, he wondered if there was a good week in November for him to fly down and "observe." I agreed to show him around as the bong made its way back in front of me.

I heard him laugh. "Are you doing a bong hit?"

"Yup," I said, trying not to lose any smoke.

He laughed again, "Perfect!" and hung up.

I was, in fact, the perfect host for a journalist—I had been at the school longer than most of the teachers and knew everyone there was to know. Also, silence makes me uncomfortable, so I talk to fill dead air. Little did I know, I was about to become the subject of a six-and-a-half-page article in *Rolling Stone*.

Soon everyone would learn that I skipped class, smoked weed, drank excessively, threw outrageous parties, didn't wear condoms, and was willing to shit in public if it meant winning an election—all details I poured onto the writer. At the time I was just hoping one of these stories would make it into the article, maybe followed by a flattering picture that I could frame on my wall to remind me of my college experience. I never could have expected what was to follow. My dad was the first one to call me, at 8 A.M. on April 1, 1997.

"What the fuck did you do? I have news people camped out in front of our house, and the phone is ringing off the hook."

As if straight out of a movie (and soon it would become one: National Lampoon's *Van Wilder*, even though it didn't end up resembling my life much at all), the doorbell rang. With the phone still in my hand, and my dad still shouting on the other end of the line, I opened the door to a UPS man holding the most important parcel I'd ever receive: my issue of *Rolling Stone*. I hung up with my dad, plopped down on the couch, and flipped to the article titled, "The Undergraduate."

The first paragraph literally brought tears to my eyes. Of all the emotions that ran through my heart that day, the one that held anchor was pride—pride that I had honestly portrayed what life at FSU had been like.

And FSU had been a dream to me. I had wanted to attend since I visited as a junior in high school and was blown away by how beautiful the campus was. University of Florida was flat, spread out, and too clean, like a ninth-grade girl with daddy issues. University of Central Florida was too new and barely had alumni. University of Miami was in god-awful Miami. But FSU was lush, rich, colorful, full of hills. At UF, UCF, or USF, you needed a car to get from class to class, an idea I wasn't into. At FSU, where the female undergrads outnumbered the men three to one, all you needed to get by was basic conversation skills.

My first day on campus, I fell in love nine times, made five new friends, got drunk, got high, and managed to go to orientation. That first semester, I passed all my classes with only minimal attendance and effort. And that became my credo: Take the classes that people told you were easy, show up when need be, and party. I won't say all the kids who attended FSU were only there to party, but all the kids *I* knew were there for the exact same reason: to have a good time and get a college degree.

I learned to drink . . . a lot. I also learned that when drinking, I could make people laugh, and often found myself at the head of a table. I enjoyed being the center of attention, the life of the party. By the time *Rolling Stone* found me, I had developed a reputation as the guy you *had* to party with.

After the article came out, things got weird. It's hard to picture now, with reality TV making the outrageous seem so mundane, but in 1997 with no precedent like Snooki or Honey Boo Boo, a college kid talking candidly about living a carefree life of excess got the media's attention. TV shows came to Tallahassee to meet me, radio stations called every fifteen minutes from as far away as Australia, ESPN sent a pre-*Jackass* Johnny Knoxville to party with me on a tour bus, and for one semester, I was truly famous in the town I cherished. As I sat next to recently drafted running back Warrick Dunn during graduation, talking about our big future plans for our now famous selves, I thought to myself, *I must be the luckiest man in the world.*

What I didn't know then was that one of my writing teachers had overheard someone making the (false) claim that I had a book deal with Random House, and that he had therefore decided to fail me out of spite. Having spent six and a half years working the system, I knew it was almost unheard of to fail a graduating senior. So the next week, I went to the instructor's office and made the plea the administration office had informed me was necessary.

He stopped me mid-sentence. "I don't give a shit, you can go fuck yourself. I'm not gonna help you. You have skipped through life without a care in the world and succeeded. Now you have a movie deal, a book deal, a stand-up comedy career . . . you're famous, why do you need a college degree? Go out to Hollywood and make your millions."

"But I'm only three credits short and yours is a creative writing class, it's a subjective grade . . . or objective. I always get those mixed up."

He didn't laugh. He leaned forward in his chair and seethed, "I've been writing my whole adult life and I take it very seriously. And here you come—blacking out, smoking pot, shitting, skipping classes, and you get a book deal? And, to make things even worse, you and your party lifestyle have sullied the very university I am trying to get my degree from. I will never pass you. I'm not going to help you, and there's nothing you can do to change my mind. Please leave my office."

Dumbstruck, I walked out of his office and left Florida State for good. As it turned out, it was the best thing that ever happened to me. I moved to New York to start a career in stand-up comedy that has taken me around the world and onto stages in places I could have never imagined.

First, however, at the insistence of my father, I had to enroll (via correspondence) in what turned out to be the two hardest classes I had ever taken. These were pre-Internet classes, just a box of books and a test sent to me through the State of Florida, the same classes given to inmates at correctional facilities. In the end, I managed to get the credits I needed to get my degree, and today I sit here, a forty-year-old college graduate (barely), sincerely wondering: What if I had studied harder? What if I had partied less, taken life more seriously, not fucked around at every opportunity, and focused more on academics like every teacher I ever had told me I should?

I'm not sure what the answer is, but I can say with 100 percent certainty that had I been more serious and more focused, I wouldn't be doing what I do now: making people laugh for a living. I wouldn't be selling out comedy clubs, I wouldn't be appearing regularly on radio and television, and I definitely wouldn't be hosting my own TV shows. I would have never robbed a train with the Russian mafia, swam with great white sharks, fought a bear, played arena football, been mauled by a bull, jumped out of an airplane with Rachael Ray, partied with David Lee Roth, or thrown Johnny Knoxville down a flight of stairs.

I would have absolutely nothing to write about, and maybe I'd be just as bitter as the teacher who told me to go fuck myself fifteen years ago.

I don't remember that teacher's name, but I hope he is still sitting in his tiny closet of an office, reading this paragraph. He definitely remembers me, and if by chance you are reading this: Teacher, I hope this book makes you angry beyond belief, and frustrated that you never got out of Tallhassee and lived a life worth writing about. And even more angry knowing full well that I just misspelled Tallahassee.

1.

Worthy Keeper of the Annals

I've never suffered from stage fright. As a matter of fact I suffer from the exact opposite of stage fright. I suffer from the fear of not getting on stage, of not grabbing the spotlight, of letting a potentially magical moment slip by. I'm not sure what drives it, nor am I sure how to control it, all I know is that I will give a three count of noble "*no's*" before I risk making a complete ass out of myself.

"Bert, you should get up there and say something!"

"No." *One.*

"Seriously, the mic is open."

"I think it's a bad idea." *Two.*

"It would be hilarious . . ."

"Really?" *Three.*

"Yeah . . ."

And I'm off. There have been some beauties and some beasts (more often than not beasts). And it's those ugly ones that are generally remembered the longest.

But there have been a handful of beauties, too. . . .

One of my earliest recollections is entering first grade. I had a very hard time with separation anxiety my first week. I'd previously gone to a school where my mom taught and my sister attended, so I don't think I had a firm grasp of what entering first grade entailed—the inherent gravity of it. It dawned on me when I got in my dad's van that morning, and we left for school—alone. As we merged onto the interstate and into traffic, I felt my stomach swirl. I was in the system. My dad, like everyone else on the road, was thinking about the traffic. But for me, the fact that I was alone with my dad felt odd. We hadn't spent a lot of time alone up until then. I was still too young, and he was working a lot.

He must have noticed my unease, because halfway to school he asked me what was going on.

"Nothing."

"Are you sure?"

"Do you think it would be okay for you not to go to work today and maybe hang out with me at my new school?"

"I'll hang out for a while, but I'm going to have to go to work at some point."

"Maybe you could just skip work and hang out, like, outside the classroom."

"I think they have rules against that, buddy."

We went back and forth like this all the way to my new school, up the stairs, and into my classroom, where I began to melt down. This is the parenting job my dad pulled on me:

"Here's the deal: I won't go anywhere. I will sit in the parking lot all day in my van until you're done with school. If you need me, just come out to the parking lot and get me."

And I believed him—for the first ten minutes of first grade. It was then that I politely informed my teacher, Mrs. Thompson, that I would be taking a little break from the introductory portion of today's lesson and heading out to the parking lot. I explained that I had just about had my fill of being without my family and needed to find my dad, who had promised to wait in his van in case such a situation were to arise. She explained in her soft Southern accent that my dad had gone to work. He was not in the parking lot. I was going nowhere.

To say I took this news poorly is like saying DMX has some bumps on his driving record.

Tears turned into sobs, which turned into panic, which turned into sheer panic, which turned into mayhem. I made my way from desk to desk, from kid to kid, explaining that we might never see our parents again. Mrs. Thompson had lost control, and her only hope was to get me on her side to help calm the kids down. So we made a pact: I would do first grade peacefully, as long as I got to sit at the front of the class, my desk next to her, holding her hand.

What can I tell you, I'm a straight-up gangster.

That year I discovered the band KISS, and with that discovery, found my life's direction. Whenever I could, I dressed in as much drag as I could pull together from my mom's closet, threw on as much makeup as I could sneak, and performed solo renditions, earphones on, in our living room. "Shout It Out Loud" was my preferred jam, although "Rock And Roll All Nite" inspired some stellar solo performances.

A couple of my uncles were living with us at the time, trying to start a band, and they would go wild with laughter at my one-man show, which I couldn't hear (due to the headphones). They would suggest dance moves, wardrobe choices, and mock guitar licks, for my benefit and their amusement. I jumped at the coaching, following their direction to a T. Come Christmas, I was a goddamned air-guitaring Jimi Hendrix.

So you can imagine the excitement that overwhelmed me when I first caught wind of our elementary-school talent show. Finally, all my training could be put to use. I almost felt bad for the kids who had to muster together some kind of performance in a matter of weeks, while I had been in rehearsals since August. I kept a lid on my project, though, and practiced even more dutifully than before. I listened more closely to my uncles' guidance, as they sipped their Heinekens. I kept my eye on the prize.

Come talent-show morning I was ready. I told my mom the night before that I had entered and would need to borrow some of her clothes. My mom, hands down the most supportive woman I know, didn't offer the least resistance. She dressed me to the nines. I would handle my own hair and makeup. My mom walked me through what to put on and how to apply it. (I had to pretend that I hadn't been putting on her makeup in secret for months.)

I met my dad at the front door for school that morning shirtless, in my mom's panty hose, with chains draped across my chest, cowboy boots, a cape, and a tote bag full of product.

My dad blinked. "What the fuck is this?"

"I have a talent show today and this is my costume."

"Does your mother know about this?"

"She dressed me!"

"Of course she did."

After he conferred with my mom for a minute, we drove silently for twenty-five minutes to downtown Tampa. In hindsight, I imagine my dad acted with me the same way he would if he had to, say, give a transvestite a ride home. But at the time I thought nothing of it. I was already envisioning my future glory. As I got out of the car, my dad handed me a bag.

"I had your mom pack an extra set of clothes and your uniform just in case you . . . got cold." I took the bag, thanked him, and was on my way. I could hardly wait for the reception I would get from my first-grade class.

The school day went just fine, as I remember it. I distinctly remember not being nervous but excited. Funny, too, because now, as a professional performer, I always get nervous. But that day I was stone-cold confident: I was going to murder.

Then, suddenly, it was time for the talent show. Mrs. Thompson allowed my classmate Brian Callahan and me to go to the bathroom to take care of my hair and makeup. Ten minutes later we were back, and I was Gene Simmons. The class circled me admiringly. I couldn't wait to see the looks on their faces after my performance. I'd be a god.

We left as a class for the auditorium, and I split off with Brian, who had now assumed the role of tour manager. We learned that I'd be performing in the latter half of the show. So I settled in, waiting for my cue as Brian made his way back to sit with the class.

The show consisted of a predictable assortment of gymnastics, piano, comedy, and juggling. It wasn't until about halfway through that I saw him. A fourth grader with a violin—dressed as KISS lead guitarist Ace Frehley. My heart sank—this kid had stolen my act. He walked up to me and nodded.

"Which one are you supposed to be?"

"Gene Simmons."

"Nice. What are you going to do?"

"'Rock And Roll All Nite.'"

"No, what instrument are you going to play?"

I looked at him like he had started speaking in Swahili. "Nothing," I told him.

"Nothing? What, are you . . . just going to dance?"

"Kind of."

He started laughing and walked away. It wasn't until I saw my act in this light that I realized how ill prepared I was for this *talent* show. I didn't really have a talent, per se. All these people were dazzling the masses with actual skills they possessed, had been working on, crafting. My only real talent, as I saw it, was that I liked KISS.

Panic set in as I watched Ace Frehley take the stage. Just seeing his makeup was enough to set off the crowd. Great, my one sure bet and he just stole it. Ace then banged out a semirecognizable version of "Shout It Out Loud." He closed with a mock guitar strum on his violin. The place went nuts.

He passed me without a word as he left the stage, then went over to the other fourth graders and slapped them five (high fives weren't around yet). A couple of kids went on in between us and as they did, I felt the pressure mounting and my confidence wilting. I had no act, my costume looked ridiculous, my makeup was suspect. And I realized that I had somehow completely overlooked the "hair" portion of my hair-and-makeup routine.

But there was no time to do anything about it. It was showtime. I had them start the music before my entrance, just as I would do with my uncles. But with no instrument to show for myself, the crowd was more confused than anything. I can only imagine they were trying to figure out what this mini drag queen had in store.

It's moments like these that define a man—when he must choose between risking major, public humiliation or admit that he's been outclassed. I took that moment to sprint and then slide onto my knees up to the very edge of the stage.

I then proceeded to air-guitar the fuck out my song for the K-through-Five set.

The build started at the back, the fifth graders who I'm sure had been rolling their eyes at the kid with the violin. After all the pianos, violins, and jugglers, to then have a first grader crank a song they all knew and loved and get *weird as fuck* on their asses—it must have been a treat. I jammed for the whole song. Students sang along with me as I belted out the lyrics as loud as I could.

I don't remember too much of what followed. There was the looks on their faces. The sounds of their cheers.

But mainly I remember the elation of having been on stage. When my parents picked me up at school, I wasn't the same kid who had been dropped off that morning. I didn't enter the talent show the next year, the year after that, or any other years at elementary school, but one thing was for sure: the bug of performing had bitten me.

They haven't all been beauties. For every beauty, there are a dozen beasts. Fast-forward to 1993, Florida State University.

By this time in my life I had begun to make a name for myself as a Funny Guy. I would write comic songs on my guitar about our friends, I was quick with a joke or a comeback, and was the go-to dude when our fraternity needed to put together a sketch or a skit. People would introduce me as one of the funniest guys they knew, and every once in a while, someone would pull me aside and tell me in all seriousness that I should try my hand at being a comedian.

It sounded beyond unattainable, so I stayed in my small circle, continuing to make my friends laugh. My fraternity was the one place I knew I could always draw an audience. There were a few times a year when all 180 of us would gather, and one of those was elections. Guys would prepare a speech, put on a coat and tie, draw up bullet points on poster paper, and go around the room trying to sway votes in their direction.

The more ambitious among us saw this as an opportunity to grow, network, pad a resume. I found it an ideal time to mock those guys. You got ten minutes to win votes. These were my ten minutes to entertain, my first brushes with stand-up. The first year I sang a song, got huge laughs—and lost. The second year, I gave a very sincere ten-minute speech, completely naked. At first I got laughs, then very uncomfortable eye contact as I strutted around the stage pretending not to be naked. My platform was, "I have nothing to hide," and despite my command performance, I lost again.

The third year I hadn't prepared anything when I saw that Josh Young was running uncontested for the position of Worthy Keeper of the Annals. I had been taking myself really seriously at the time. I was in a band, plotting a path away from Writer-Comedian and toward Brooding Artist. But old habits die hard. My bandmate, John Dacre, leaned over to me and whispered, "Are you going to run against him?"

"No." *One.*

"Are you going to run at all?"

"I don't think so." *Two.*

"Well, you can't let him run uncontested, you gotta go up there naked again."

"To be honest my stomach is kind of bothering me; if I did go up there, I would probably just shit all over the place." *Three.*

Having heard only the last half of the conversation, our bassist and John's best friend, Brent Brackin, chimed in. "That would be hilarious! You have to do that!"

I looked to Dacre, waiting for somebody to back down, but his eyes had widened.

"Yeah, you're doing that!"

And just like that it was decided.

The two stood up and, in unison, said, "We nominate Bert Kreischer for the Worthy Keeper of the Annals."

"Bert," our president said, "do you accept?"

I reluctantly nodded. The three of us headed back to the bathroom to prepare for my speech.

Worthy Keeper of the Annals, the unfortunately titled office I was running for, was fairly low on the ballot, which meant it came early—and that we had very little time to plan anything. Lucky for us, the speech as we conceived it required very little preparation. I stripped nude, Brackin found a tie for me, and Dacre, in a moment of genius, pulled an empty pizza box out of the garbage. The president came back to the bathroom to see if we were ready. We were.

We walked in toward the end of Josh's speech, for which he was wielding a laser pointer (brand-new technology for the early 1990s). He was in a suit and tie, and closed with something to the effect of, "And that is why I think you should vote for me."

Josh took a seat as Brackin walked into the room and

began to speak on my behalf, the kind of endorsement every candidate was required to have.

He started solemnly, "Guys, as you know Bert can be something of a jokester, a prankster if you will. But ever since we started our band, I've seen a very different side of him. And I think tonight, if you look past the Bert you have come to know, you, too, will see a different side of him. With that said, for the position of Worthy Keeper of the Annals, our brother, Bert Kreischer."

Dacre discreetly slid the pizza box into place. I revealed myself to the crowd, wearing only a tie. Like last year, they went nuts. A little lightheartedness was welcome, in what had come to be very serious and sometimes unhealthy campaigning. I walked up to the pizza box, butt cheeks clenched, and waited for the crowd to calm down.

"I would like to show you all a very different side of me," I said, turning my back to the crowd, facing the previous year's council. The audience laughed at what they thought was a simple joke: my ass. But as I let go, I heard a gasp.

It was the sound of the last breaths of fresh air in the room behind inhaled.

The council, sitting at their designated table, seemed confused at first. I started peeing at their feet. (As we all learned that day, you can't go number two without a little number one.)

The smell was absolutely atrocious. The room cleared

out in a matter of seconds. People literally jumped out of the windows, piled out of every door, began violently dry-heaving. The council lost their minds and demanded that I go back in the room and clean up my mess, which I did (and directly after, threw up). I'll spare you too much description except to say that my aim for the pizza box was balls-on accurate.

We gave the room a solid ten minutes of aerosol air freshener, assumed our places, and waited for everyone to vote. Ballots were collected as Josh and I stood at the front of the room, listening as people chuckled over what they had just seen. As the votes were tallied, I heard a rumbling of dissent from the members.

"You guys have got to be fucking kidding right now."

We answered with curious faces.

"There is only one vote for Josh. Bert won in a landslide."

The place went fucking bananas. Josh walked over to the ballots and confirmed what the council had told us, that everyone had voted for me . . . except for his own vote, for himself. (I had opted to abstain, as I found both candidates incompetent. I instead wrote, "Mills Sucks Pole" on my ballot.)

The council congratulated me as Josh began to shout. "You're not really gonna let this happen are you? The guy shit on a pizza box! I have a plan and a laser pointer. I wore a fucking suit."

"He won fair and square," said the president.

Josh looked at his brethren and shouted, "This is fucking bullshit!"

An unknown brother piped back, "No, it's bertshit."

If these two stories, the beauty and the beast, form my
legacy as an entertainer, then so be it. I hope to keep
growing artistically, and I think these stories suggest I
have. But if, at my funeral, the only people to speak are
my makeup artist Brian Callahan and my bandmates
John Dacre and Brent Brackin, and they share these two
stories with the friends and family in attendance, please
know that I will be smiling from up above. Naked. In KISS
makeup. Rocking the fuck out.

2.

Alcoholism, Vandalism, Drug Use, and Other Ways to Have a Good Time

Fraternities take a lot of flak, and rightly so. Mine was something of a breeding ground for racism, sexism, alcoholism, vandalism, homophobia, and drug use. I know that anyone with a liberal blog is about to lose their mind and get those angry butterflies that inhabit enraged chests, but my goal here is not to anger, but to show you how much fun racism, alcoholism, vandalism, homophobia, and drug use can be for a young man. Maybe shine a light on a secret part of society, the way a disco ball sparkles in a dorm room at 3 A.M. when you're blowing up on X. No one ever meant too much harm. We were a bunch of

simple-minded boys who were desperately trying to find
out who we were before entering the big wide world. There's
a part of me that wishes I had been strong enough as a
young man to carve my own path, rather than following
in the footsteps of so many. But it was a whole lot of fucking fun if you were a guy with six years to kill. One thing
I can say for certain, I would do it again completely.

I pledged along with my roommate and best friend at
the time, Jeff Hartley, in the fall of 1991, the first semester of my freshman year, the year grunge meandered its
flannels onto the music scene. We rushed a couple fraternities but gravitated toward the one that was populated
mostly by guys who had gone to our high school in Tampa.
Pledging a fraternity is a mindfuck of an activity. They
wine and dine you to get you to join, then allow you a
two- to three-week grace period, just enough for you to
get comfortable. It's the kind of grace period an abusive
husband or a sociopath might give you. You're comfortable, you're confident, then when you least expect it, you
are hiding in the closet because you've overcooked dinner.
The first time it happened to me was also the first time I
heard the N-word used unapologetically. I was so appalled
I almost stood up and left. But no one else was leaving,
and considering that the group of older boys yelling at us
was looking for someone to single out—and standing up
and protesting, *"Language, gentlemen,"* would do exactly
that—I held in my liberal rage until we were alone.

After the meeting my pledge class sat around in a circle drinking beers, collecting our thoughts. I waited for the right moment to voice my concern.

"Can you believe that guy said the N-word?"

"Grow the fuck up," said one of my older pledge brothers, who had gotten hazed beyond belief and would later de-pledge because of it. "He didn't mean it as racist. He wasn't calling a *black person* a nigger. He was calling *us* niggers; it's not racist if you call a white person a nigger." Although I cringed every time he said the word, you couldn't argue with his logic.

Another pledge brother chimed in. "Yeah, it had nothing to do with race . . . you dumb nigger."

Everyone laughed, and I left my longhaired liberal outrage behind. And that is how complicity to racism happens.

It made sense in a way. They were constantly trying to shock us. In that climate, you kind of fell into line quickly and you were never comfortable. Anytime you felt relaxed, it was because they let you feel relaxed so you could slip up just enough that they could haze you. They were giving you the rope to hang yourself. They'd let you show your ass and then call you on it. So when they did haze you, it was for those things that you'd done—like admit which brother you thought didn't belong in the fraternity, or who had the hottest chick you'd like to fuck, or better yet who you thought might be gay. The proper reprimand would always involve ratting you out and lots of screaming.

To say that our house was a place of hazing is like saying that Guantánamo Bay is a residence for independent-thinking Middle Easterners. There were one or two guys that got hazed worse than the others because people had personal beefs with them. I got hazed because I was gullible, likeable, and something of a moron. I'd be walking into the house in the early morning to clean the up head and pass Pete Whalen, a guy I'm still friends with. He'd see me walk in, tired and hungover, and grab hold of me.

"Hey, at 6 A.M. I need you to wake up Brother Siminson."

"Seriously?"

"Yeah, he asked me to do it, but I have to leave."

"What do you want me to do?"

"He's a heavy sleeper, so he said to grab a hammer and bang on his door until he gets up."

"Are you sure?"

"Certain. And don't make me say it again, pledge. You got a dip?"

Dip was the binding powder that brought us all closer to each other. Ground-up tobacco that you pinched and placed between your bottom lip and teeth. Your safety as a pledge was dependent on two things: if you dipped, and what brand you dipped. The only two acceptable brands were Skoal mint and Copenhagen. Copenhagen was for the guys who owned trucks, had been hit by their fathers, drank whiskey, and said the N-word. Skoal mint was for the softer boys, who usually came from country clubs, private schools, and veered away from racial slurs. Pete and I were Skoal men, as was Siminson. I pulled out a fresh can, handed it to Pete, and he took a big morning-sized dip, as did I.

"So, I'm safe leaving my responsibility in your hands?"

"Safe!"

"I don't want to get fucked on this one!"

"You won't, I promise." We both spat and walked in separate directions, me to clean the up head, and Pete to economics class.

Come 6 A.M., there I was with a framing hammer outside Siminson's door. I started soft, but after a short while found no result. My soft taps then turned into harder bumps, grouped in machine-gun spurts. Still nothing. Slowly I could hear other brothers in other rooms waking up, shouting for the guy with the jackhammer to stop, but still I heard nothing from my intended target. Finally, I decided to pull the stops and began taking Paul Bunyan-sized swings at my target. The dip juice seeped between my teeth as I swung at the door with all my might. I remembered thinking at one point I should probably pull back a bit or I might just knock the numbers off, when I finally heard movement in his room. Excited, like a fisherman who feels a tug on his line and wants to set his hook, I banged out a few murderous booms for good measure, and with that Siminson was at the door, in a rage.

"What the fuck are you doing?"

"You have to wake up."

Siminson looked still asleep but shocked, like someone had just lit him on fire in the middle of his slumber. He grabbed the hammer out of my hand and slammed the door in my face. "Motherfucker," I heard him yell from the other side of the door.

Part of me wanted to make sure he was up, and the other part of me realized Pete had most likely been fucking with me. The question of which part of me was right was answered when I ran into Siminson at lunch in the mess hall.

"I'm gonna make your life a living fucking hell this semester."

"But Brother Siminson, Brother Whalen—"

"Shut the fuck up before I go to my room, get that hammer, and shove it up your ass. You got a dip?"

I handed him my can of Skoal, he put it in his pocket and walked away. That was the way it worked. Brothers fucked with the pledges, and if they could ricochet it so that fucking with us meant fucking with a brother at the same time, even better.

One night, I was setting up the mess hall for dinner when I got called into the kitchen by one of the older brothers called Cuz. Cuz was from the Panhandle, and he had the kind of happy-go-lucky attitude that made everyone like him. A couple years later he would go on to work for Nabisco and show up at my house with rejected boxes of cookies, and we would get stoned and feast on broken Nutter Butters. But back then he was just a brother working in the kitchen to help pay his dues. And I was his pledge.

Cuz was hollowing out pumpkins for a pumpkin-carving social we had with a sorority later that night, and when I walked into the kitchen he had his hands full of pumpkin innards.

"Yo, Bert. You take a look out there and tell me if there is anyone wearing a suit."

I looked out and noticed that, in fact, there were quite a few brothers wearing suits. I told him so and he smiled.

"Do me a favor and reset the tables for an outside dinner."

"Okay!" I said. The word *no* has never been a strong part of my vocabulary.

I got all the tables on the basketball courts and set out all the plates. When I came back in he had an even bigger smile on his face.

"Bert, you wanna play a hilarious prank on the brothers? I mean this is a legendary, next-level kind of prank that will be talked about for years, just like the donut prank."

The donut prank had occurred a few years earlier and

was the stuff of folklore. The pledges at the time, after spending a night getting hazed beyond belief by irate and drunk brothers, woke up early the next morning and left the brothers a couple dozen donuts in the lounge as a peace offering.

The brothers woke up, hungover, and feasted on them. Later that day the pledges posted a blow-up picture of themselves in the same lounge, with the same donuts, only with them skewered on their dicks. The brothers got pissed, but the prank was so legendary it was worth it. And that was the ultimate job of the pledge class: to grow enough balls to prank the brothers.

"Will they get pissed?"

"No, come here." He led me into the storage closet. "Take all this flour up to the roof and hide. When they start saying grace, I want you to run to the edge of the roof and throw all the flour on the brothers. Then I'll come out and spray them with the hose and yell, 'Looks like ya'll got the ol' papier-mâché treatment!'"

Cuz started laughing so hard at the idea of his prank that the laughter became contagious, and soon we are both smiling ear to ear. I was already figuring out the dance I'd do up on the roof afterward, kind of a mix of the Ed Lover Dance and the Icky Shuffle. He told me to grab Accardi, the only other guy to get hazed as much as me—if not worse—and to get on the roof through the only access we had: Brother Bongwater's window. After we dumped the flour, we'd go back into his room and hide until it all blew over. He said if there was any fallout, he would take it for us. But when time passed and everyone realized just how funny the ol' papier-mâché incident was, we would get full credit, and it would become legend.

Accardi and I grabbed four sacks of flour, went to Brother Bongwater's room, locked the door behind us, climbed onto the roof, and waited like snipers. Many a thought passed through our heads while we waited, including, "Is this a good idea?" and "Is this really how you make papier-mâché?" and "Will everyone know that this was how you make papier-mâché?" and "What does *mâché* mean?" and "Why exactly is this so funny to Cuz?" But when we heard Cuz start off dinner by announcing, "Brothers, please. A moment of prayer," we leapt into action like soldiers. I covered the near side and Accardi dumped the brothers on the far side. We thrilled at coating the brothers who'd hazed us the most, waiting for Cuz to come out with the hose.

What happened wasn't what was planned. Instead of Cuz, one of our pledge brothers showed up with a hose, and he proceeded to shower our suited brothers.

Cuz stood by his side feigning astonishment.

"What have they done? The balls on these guys to hit you with the ol' papier-mâché treatment." He turned his gaze toward us. "Look, on the roof, it's Kreischer and

Accardi! They're going to Bongwater's room! I'll get the keys!"

We crawled back into our only escape, eyeing each other in panic like we had been running a train on a hooker in Haiti and both our condoms simultaneously broke.

"They're gonna beat our asses."

"They're not allowed to hit us," I said hopefully.

"They hit me all the time," Accardi said.

At that we heard the keys to the door jingling outside, like a Drunk Santa coming in to discipline his unruly reindeer.

"Bert, whatever you do, don't hit them back."

The door opened and to my relief, I saw that the first to enter was the most religious brother of our fraternity. He stood, covered in flour, but I knew that without a doubt, despite being enraged, he wouldn't resort to violence.

That's when I got punched.

It turns out he had been on his way to meet his girl-friend's parents—in a suit and tie—when Cuz had asked him if he could do him a favor and hang out long enough to say the prayer, which he happily had agreed to do.

He hit me pretty squarely in the jaw, but since he was a devout Christian, it didn't really hurt. Behind him was Siminson, wearing a huge smile. Accardi immediately took a swing at him and missed. As many people as could fit in Bongwater's room jumped on us and dragged us down-stairs. So began the longest hazing session of my life.

Pumpkin innards were placed in just about any spot they could find. Brothers took turns in sort of a lazy-Susan manner hazing me, including Cuz, who I could see smiling as he did it. Then he would retreat to the back of the line and egg on the brothers covered in flour.

"You look absolutely ridiculous, he ruined your suit with the ol' papier-mâché trick . . . *no respect!*"

We stood our ground and didn't say a word for fear that it would only make things worse and because no one would believe us.

I wasn't really sure why Cuz did it to us—just fucking with someone for fuck's own sake, I guess. But I did notice the next time I saw him, it was as though we shared a secret. He never hazed me again, even treated me like something of a friend, if not exactly an equal.

And that was how we were taught to bond: by treating each other horribly and sharing a laugh about it later. It's like the Friars Club motto, "We only Roast the ones we love." The more you liked someone, the further you could take it.

When it was my turn, it was a great feeling to set up a pledge you liked and watch the result. Like lightly covering the mouth of a bong in shoe polish and offering a pledge a bong hit during Hell Week. Hell Week was the week at the end of the semester, just before the pledges were about to be made brothers, when all the hazing was crammed into 120 sleepless, drunken hours. We'd get

one of them high with the ol' shoe-polish trick and watch
as he walked around the house with a brown ring around
his lips. Or we'd discreetly ask a pledge for a glass of
water during an important meeting, then wait till he was
gone to yell to the masses, "Can you believe this guy? He
said he wanted a water and just walked out like it was
nothing at all. If that dude comes back with a water, we
better give it to him."

Fucking with each other was an art and we got so good
at it, you would assume we hated each other. Bottle rock-
ets under a door. Yelling from a balcony to the pool at
spring break, "Kaiser, you forgot to put on your butt-rash
medicine," or passing a guy on campus who was standing
with a hot chick and greeting him with, "Damn, you have
a new chick every time I see you!"

By the time I was a sophomore I was out of the dorms and
a full-fledged brother of my fraternity. This was the first
true year of my independence. The summer before, I had
started growing out my hair and listening to Widespread
Panic. I bought a dog, an iguana, and a mountain bike.
Needless to say, I was also smoking a great deal of weed.
This was going to be the new version of Bert I presented
to the masses. The high-school athlete/meathead/finger-
fucking-in-the-back-of-a-Jetta guy was dead. Now I was
a sensitive guy with social insights and longer hair.

I moved in with two friends, Hartley and a guy we all called Cheese. The three of us had all gone to high school together, and we'd known each other since before that. Hartley was—and still is—an alpha male. But he was an alpha male with a twist. He had been a twin, and his brother died when he was ten. What that does to an average boy, I can't tell you, but I can tell you what it did to Hartley. He was a massively compassionate friend when it was just the two of you, but in groups, he was an unyielding bully. He was tall, strong, and aggressively handsome, something he was well aware of. With a blazer on he looked like a Baldwin; with a whiskey in his hand he acted like a Kennedy. He loved to fight and always won. When he saw the changes that I was making in my lifestyle, he openly mocked me. But then, privately, he asked me to help him buy a dog, an iguana, and a mountain bike.

Cheese, on the other hand, was a beta. He had known Hartley and his brother since before his brother died. Cheese would always say Hartley's brother was the true alpha of the two. He and Cheese had been close mostly because they were the biggest kids of their age. Cheese had developed before most of his peers—he was already shaving in eighth grade. But by the time we got to college, the rest of us had caught up with or even passed him in size. This either humbled him or put things into perspective, because he was a much quieter, sensitive guy by the time we were sophomores in college living together.

Hartley and I joined a fraternity, but Cheese waited to make sure his grades were up to snuff first ("like a faggot," Hartley said). So he joined the next semester, and by the time we all moved in, Hartley and I were brothers and Cheese was finishing up his pledgeship. Cheese and I hung out very easily, as I find I do with most people. Hartley and Cheese meanwhile were closer with each other than I was with either of them, but Hartley was relentlessly rough on him. I wonder if Cheese saw in Hartley the little brother he really was, and that bothered Hartley. But still, Cheese was quick to get pissed, and Hartley loved it. Cheese forgave even faster—I knew that was the reason deep down Hartley felt so comfortable fucking with him. If Hartley was a bully, Cheese was passive-aggressive to the core. Hearing one day that Hartley had a fear of snakes, Cheese promptly drove to a pet store and bought a large python. That was Cheese's way of fighting back.

On our first day in our new apartment, Hartley walked upstairs and decided who would live in what rooms.

"With the amount of pussy I get and my new dog, I'll need the room with the private bath and balcony. You two faggots can share a bathroom. Bert, you get the room on the corner 'cause you have a girlfriend, and Cheese, you get the room that looks like a closet."

Hartley agreed to pay one hundred dollars more for his better room. I took the medium one, and Cheese took all his worldly possessions—which included a big-screen

TV, a desk, wall-sized cabinets, and stereo with surround sound—and turned his closet into a personal oasis. (The only thing he left downstairs was his snake, of course.)

"The guy's got electronics worth ten grand in his room," Hartley said, "and we've got a twenty-inch TV and a goddamned alarm clock for entertainment downstairs."

"He said if we pay fifty dollars more a month, he'll leave it downstairs," I offered.

"I'm not renting his fucking entertainment system. I'll just watch TV in his room when he's not here."

Which Hartley did, often. In retaliation, Cheese would leave Hartley's dog in Hartley's room with food and water, and then shut the door behind it.

One day, Hartley walked into my room with a smile and closed my door.

"My dog shit in my room again, so . . . I greased up Cheese's brakes on his mountain bike; let's see if we can get him to do the Widowmaker with us." The Widowmaker was a steep hill near our town house, as grueling an uphill ride as it was a lightning-fast downhill one.

"We'll get him with the good-cop-bad-cop routine."

"Good-cop-bad-cop?"

"Yeah, the good cop is going up the hill . . . the bad cop is the ride down."

Not sure if that was the correct way to use that analogy, I said nothing and smiled. We walked into Cheese's room and Hartley plopped down on his bed.

"Hey, buddy, you wanna go mountain biking with us?" Hartley said.

"No, I'm gonna take a nap."

"Come on, it'll be fun."

"I said I'm gonna take a nap."

"What are you, nine months old? You want me to put socks on your hands so you don't scratch your face? Come on, man, let's go hang!"

"No!"

"Don't say no. Hang out with us. We'll go mountain biking, head over to the house, get a few cold beers, ride through campus, check out the talent, come home, shower up, and we'll go out tonight."

"You guys go. I'm gonna take a nap, and I'll go out with you later."

"Come on, dude."

"Fuck off, Hartley. I said no."

"Fine then, be a little faggot."

Defeated, Hartley and I got on our bikes, went for a ride, and retreated to our fraternity house to explain how close we got to pulling off a legendary prank. We went out that night and forgot about it.

A week later Cheese asked us to go biking. We agreed and later we all met at the peak of the Widowmaker. In typical Hartley fashion, he decided the order.

"You guys are both faggots, so I'll take the lead."

"I'll go second," I said.

"Well, I don't want you two assholes trying to ride your bikes up my ass to prove to me what a faggot you think I am. So I'm fine with the anchor," Cheese said.

"Anchor is a great way to say you're riding bitch."

"I'm riding anchor."

"Alright then, I'll see you faggots at the bottom," Hartley said, then led off fast and furious. I followed, with Cheese staying well behind to give himself an ample cushion.

I was completely on my own, flying over bumps in the trail and whistling around corners—when I heard the shrill squeal of compromised brakes, as they struggled to stop two hundred pounds of Cheese. I slowed down to look over my shoulder and that is when the gap closed. Within seconds, he'd flown past me, *Top Gun* flyby style, glancing alternately at me, his bike, and the trail. I heard him say as he blew past, "What the fuck, man, something's wrong with my bike! My fucking bike is broken!"

His pace was breakneck. I sped up thinking I could do something to help, but I couldn't catch him. Cheese was howling down the Widowmaker like he was being poured over nachos, and by the time he caught up to Hartley I was still well behind. All I heard was the smashing of tree branches and the shrieks of terror as Cheese flew off the designated path, shredded.

A minute later, I caught up to Hartley about twenty yards away from the path Cheese had just created in the flora.

"What the fuck is he doing?" Hartley said.

"We greased his brakes."

"What?"

"We greased his brakes last week and forgot about it."

Hartley's face turned from confusion to terror, then to absolute joy.

"Ohhh fuck me! I fucking forgot about that. How fucking great is this moment? It's even better this way than if we'd gotten him to go with us then."

"We would have stopped him," I said.

"You would have. I wouldn't have. But you didn't get a chance to, and that's why this is so perfect."

"He might be dead!"

"He's not. I can hear him crying in there."

Cheese emerged from the shrubbery with his bike in his hand, in pain, and enraged.

"This thing is a goddamned piece of shit!"

"What happened?" Hartley said, feigning concern. "You can't throw caution to the wind like that and ride recklessly; we care too much about you, Cheese!"

"It wouldn't stop. I was pulling the brakes as hard as I could and it wouldn't fucking stop. I could have fucking died."

"Are you hurt?" I asked timidly.

"No, I don't think so."

Cheese dropped his bike next to us on the ground and started examining it. "I just can't figure it out; it seriously wouldn't stop."

"I'd check the brakes," Hartley offered. I shot him a look, but he only smirked.

"No shit I'm gonna check the brakes." There was a pause. "What the fuck?"

Hartley started to laugh. I took a deep breath.

"There's something on my brakes."

"That can't be good," Hartley said, helpfully.

He wiped the frame of his tire and the brake pads and found substantial amounts of WD-40.

"There's fucking grease on here. Can you fucking believe that?"

"No way," Hartley said.

"How the fuck did WD-40 get on my tires and brakes?"

"Did you ride through some on your way here?"

"No."

"Do you normally grease your brakes up before a ride?"

"No."

"Did you recently grease your chain, and maybe get some on your tires?"

"No, I don't think so."

We were stumped.

"Well then, I guess the only other thing I can come up

with," Hartley said, "was that last week Bert and I greased your brakes and tried to get you to come out on a ride with us but you were being a bitch."

Cheese looked at us in confusion while what Hartley said sank in.

"And had you not taken a nap, we would have stopped the prank before you flew off the trail."

Cheese looked to me for confirmation.

"But you didn't, and we forgot, and you almost killed yourself. You only have yourself to blame, if you think about it."

"In our defense, we did forget," I said.

Silently he picked up his bike and walked up the trail, away from both of us.

Cheese was the ultimate patsy. It was as if he was setting himself up sometimes. He would buy himself something special, like a celebratory steak and a six-pack of Mickey's, leave them in the fridge, and write a note on top of all of it to the effect of, "Dear Cocksuckers, DO NOT touch this steak and six-pack. I am saving it for after finals."

He was tempting us so much that I actually stayed away from them, thinking it was a trap. But it only baited Hartley. Hartley didn't prepare much for finals themselves, let alone celebratory dinners for after they were done. One night Hartley came home with our brothers Pete and

Siminson after blowing off a night of studying at the bar. He went to the fridge and came back with three beers and the note.

"What kind of person leaves beer in a refrigerator with a note and expects it not to get drank," he bragged to the older brothers.

"He's gonna get pissed off as shit tomorrow," I thought out loud to Hartley.

"I'll fill them up with water and put the tops back on."

I said nothing in rebuttal. I was only a couple months past these two guys hazing the shit out of me, and the marks were still fresh. Hartley filled them with water, and just like the brakes, we completely forgot about it. Come Friday at 5 P.M., after Cheese's last final, as we packed our cars to head home for Christmas break and readied ourselves for the last night of partying, Cheese strolled in, triumphant.

"I've been waiting for this moment," he announced like a 1950s father coming home from work.

He started the grill and rolled back into the living room, beer in hand.

"Too bad you guys don't have any beers here to celebrate finals with, and don't even try askin', 'cause I ain't giving." Thinking nothing of it, Hartley and I paid little mind until we heard him open his first beer and take his first sip.

"Hmmm, this is a little flat."

He put the top on and shook it a bit, then reopened it. Still nothing.

"I'll drink this one last. Don't you hate it when you get a flat beer?" He walked back out of the kitchen with a brand-new Mickey's in hand. As he popped the top, Hartley looked at me and smiled. I remembered exactly what he was smiling about. Cheese took a sip of the new beer and looked up at us with the same confused expression. "This one tastes like shit, too."

"Do you think they're stale maybe?" Hartley said.

"They taste like water."

"Tap water?"

"I can kinda taste the beer but not really."

"Open another one."

Cheese did and heard nothing. He opened another and another until they were all opened.

"They must have been tampered with."

"Probably that. You should take them back and tell them you got screwed."

Cheese's eyes widened as he weighed the idea in his head.

"Or someone might have drunk them all last weekend and refilled them with water to teach you a lesson about putting beers in the fridge with a bullshit note."

Cheese's face began to build with impotent rage, knowing full well that all he could offer was an earful, and an earful wasn't going to change anything.

The last words he said to Hartley that semester were when we were packing to move out of our pigsty of a town house. Being messes of young men, all our shit was in huge piles all over the house, which we would simply grab and throw into boxes. Cheese walked into my room, where Hartley and I were talking about our game plan for packing, and he coyly smiled.

"Listen, I didn't want to say anything earlier, but my snake is missing. I looked in the cage, and I guess he got out today. While you're packing, keep an eye out for him."

Cheese shut the door and I saw that same pregnant silence in Hartley's face. He was now faced with the prospect of a resting python in every armful of laundry or each time he reached his hand into a dark space. I've never moved an apartment with more caution in my life, and poor Hartley left the majority of his stuff there for the next tenants. Suffice it to say, Cheese had the last word.

It's been twenty years now, and not too long ago I hung out with just about all of these guys. I was in Denver, and Cheese, Pete, and Siminson came to my greenroom before a show, cracking up about old stories and how much we used to fuck with each other.

Someone referred to Cheese as "Cheese" one too many times. "It's Chris, guys," he said. "I'm forty years old and I don't want to be called Cheese anymore." It was a moment of honesty, a moment of assertion for a guy we had tormented for half our lives. We left that night and promised to hang out the next time I was in Denver. I went back to my hotel to pack for an early flight to L.A.

The next morning, while waiting to go through airport security, I heard a familiar voice.

"Yo Bert!"

I turned and saw Siminson, dressed like a businessman and a father on his way to work, a grown-up in a collared shirt and khakis, rolling a carry-on bag.

"I was wondering if I was going to see you at the airport today," he said.

We talked for a bit about how great it was to hang out and catch up, all these years later, then said good-bye again and made our way to our respective terminals. I passed through security and waited for the train to my gate. The train arrived, and in typical early-Monday-morning-traveler fashion, we all filed silently on like it was 1980 in Communist Russia. The doors closed, and as the train pulled away from the terminal, I heard a voice break the silence.

"Holy shit! It's Bert the Conqueror!" a voice said, referring to my TV show.

I looked over to find the voice and found it was Siminson at the far end of the train, smiling ear to ear.

"Bert the Freakin' Conqueror on my train! You *are* Bert the Conqueror, right?"

Everyone was looking now, trying to figure out who he was talking to.

"Yup," I reluctantly answered.

"You're on the History Channel, right?"

"No, Travel Channel."

"Yeah, that's it. You ride all those roller coasters and scream like a little girl."

"And other stuff."

"But mostly roller coasters," he said for all to hear. "You mostly ride roller coasters."

"Yeah."

Siminson started grabbing people around him.

"Does anyone watch that show?"

He found only blank stares.

"No one watches that show? There is no way I'm the *only* person who has *ever* seen that show? This must be its first season, right?"

"Second," I again reluctantly offered, knowing full well he knew it was my second season.

"Second season? Wow, and *no one* on this train recognizes this guy at all?"

I waited, hoping someone would save me from the friendly game of humiliation, but as I looked around I could see there was no one to come to my rescue.

The other passengers were kind of enjoying trying to figure out who I was. One guy joined in. "I watch that network all the time, and I never seen this guy in my life."

"You ride roller coasters on TV?" another passenger asked. "Are you, like, a roller-coaster designer or something?"

"No, he's scared of them," Siminson said. "And he screams like a girl the whole time."

Now everyone was looking at me.

Siminson kept it up for the remainder of the ride. The train stopped at the first stop, thankfully mine. As I exited, Siminson rallied the train for a final good-bye.

"Have a safe flight, Bert the Conqueror!"

"You, too, big guy," I said. "Keep watching my show."

The doors closed behind me and I exhaled as I heard one last, "Bert the freakin' Conqueror."

As I often do in airports, I went straight to the nearest bar. I began texting all of our mutual friends to tell them how I had just been expertly punked by Siminson—when a stranger approached me from behind.

"Man, that guy must love your show," he said.

"Yeah, well, I actually know him."

"Seriously? Oh, that's too funny. I gotta say something to him next time I see him. I think my kids go to the same school as his kids. They just moved here."

"Really," I said.

"Yeah, small world. How do you know him?"

"We used to date."

"Oh."

The stranger chose not to sit down and walked away.

I'll never know if my message ever made it back to Siminson. I hope it hasn't and is just being passed around parent to parent behind his back. Maybe it's not, but it was worth a try.

3.

OOPS: A Love Story

The first time I ever felt up a girl was in seventh-grade study hall, in front of three other classmates, two of whom were girls. It was Truth or Dare, and I was dared to feel up Gwen Cohen. She giggled, I giggled, and the others looked at me as if I were a god holding a golden tit. I walked out of that classroom a man. A few minutes later I realized that my sexual conquest wasn't so much a conquest as it was a forfeiture of land. Gwen had been dared to let me feel her up and I had been dared to do it. I was no god, more a false prophet. Still, it was amazing fodder for middle-school gossip. By the end of the school day, everyone, including my teachers, knew what had happened. I watched my newfound manhood turn into boyhood humiliation as they told my mom in the parking lot while I waited in the car. Needless to say that was the longest car ride home ever.

A year later I was on a trip to Disney World, on the haunted-house ride, with a new girl. I'd heard boys brag about fingering girls plenty of times but had never really heard the details, how they went about it, the logistics. And so when I got down to business on that ride, I felt like a World War II soldier dropped on Omaha Beach without ever having seen either combat training . . . or a beach. I spent the majority of the time surveying the perimeter, taking in just how beautiful the beachfront property was, looking for a path to the beach rather than storming said beach. I found the path a lot lower than I expected it to be. When it was time to act, I invaded that beach—and stayed. I remained there, not moving at all, for the rest of the ride, staring at her awkwardly as if I were taking her temperature. That night I told no one what had happened, having learned my lesson. I was also overly concerned that I had somehow acquired testicular cancer throughout the night, because my testicles throbbed in pain. That was my first case of blue balls.

After sinking my hands in the sand, I realized it was time to go surfing. I graduated eighth grade and moved on to an all-boys Catholic high school, where losing your virginity was as mandatory as avoiding sexual contact with the priests. Sean Hooker and Ty Rodriguez had already had sex, and they held court at our lunchroom tables, explaining the fundamentals. First and foremost, you needed protection—because apparently AIDS was running rampant throughout the ninth grade. Second, you needed to find a girl from a public school. Catholic-school girls were prudes, and their parents cared about them way too much for them to ever give up their virginity to us.

So, like a nineteen-year-old with a pound of cheap weed to sell, the public schools were where I set my sights. I very quickly started dating a girl named Alison Williams, who my friends had known from their middle-school years. She was pretty in a duchess kind of way, not that I knew that at the time. What I knew at the time was she had tits and that is all that mattered. We dated for what seemed like a lifetime (roughly two months), and though I tried to find a crack in her morals, they remained more or less intact. I tried my hardest to break her like a settler tries to break a wild stallion. But the call of the wild was too strong with this one, so I left her on her mountaintop. My attempts to get her to succumb to sex were mostly made over the phone. Let's not forget I was in ninth grade. My best work involved surreptiously asking her about virginity, her virginity, how she felt about her virginity, did she know anyone who had lost theirs, and how they felt about it. She told me her best friend Jenny Powers had lost hers already and it had been a good experience, so like a gentleman, I dumped Alison and started dating her best friend, Jenny Powers—not the coolest move, I realize now. But at fifteen, a man has to do what a man has to do.

Jenny Powers, it was rumored, had had sex with upwards of two people. The most recent guy was dead set on keeping her. But I had broken up with Alison for Jenny, and Jenny broke up with the guy that loved her, and she and I started dating. I'm not quite sure what the shelf life of a ninth grader's virginity is supposed to be, once he's dating a girl, but at the time I ballparked it at about a week.

Our first night together was at a party at the aptly named Jason Stoner's house. It was a public school party and though I was a Catholic-school boy, my friends had gone to school with these kids, so I figured it would be cool for me to crash. Then she directed my attention to her ex-boyfriend, Chris, who charged me like I had just tied his nuts. Like a rodeo clown and a bull, I spent the next hour dodging errant swings and the drunken stumbling of a heartbroken ninth grader—a boy who had been given the body of a fighter but not the coordination or heart. Not wanting to start a fight, especially in the company of a bunch of dudes who knew him and not me, Jenny and I made a hasty retreat and ended up at an abandoned house two doors down. It should be noted that by now it was mid-December, and although mid-December in Florida is not that cold, to Floridians it's icy. I held her hand and romantically walked her into the vacant garage. I laid her down on the cement, moving some boards and nails, dusting away all the wood shavings so as to let her have a clean place to lie. There I began my magic. Foreplay at that time consisted of fifteen seconds of kissing, feeling up, and feeling down, all in the name of trying to get my dick out as quickly as possible. All of which I did. Only I had no protection. All our condoms were in the possession of a friend and fellow Catholic-school boy, Cayman, the guy who got me into the party. He was, at that moment, busy trying to figure out how Jason had earned his surname.

I quickly weighed my options. Unprotected sex wasn't an option (because of the AIDS outbreak in the ninth grade), so we could play with each other's bodies and not have sex. Or I could risk my own safety, sneak back into the party, and find Cayman and get a condom from him.

Needless to say, I chose the latter. Jenny accompanied me as I walked back to the party, assuring me that Chris had calmed down by now. When I arrived, I saw Chris again, who decided to prove her wrong and come after me one last time. By now he had sobered up somewhat, despite my friend Cayman's best attempts at keeping him fucked up. This time his punches were coming too close for my comfort. It being late and being fourteen, the surrounding crowd was in the mood for a fight, so my fellow

Catholic-school boys and I retreated together, my boy-hood, sadly, still intact.

The remainder of my freshman and sophomore years were spent trying to find girls, in particular, girls who had been rumored to have had sex with boys. There was Michelle, Jenny, Jennifer, Jen, another Jennifer, and yet another Jen. Come junior year I had been driving for over twelve months and I felt like my time was well overdue. I had to either lose my virginity or accept the fact that I might be gay. That's when I met and fell in love with a girl I will simply call The Saint.

The Saint was Italian, and had had sex with two guys, which in my mind meant I was a shoo-in. I tactfully consulted my best friend, Jeff, and he confirmed the information. He played on the varsity football team, and being the gentlemen they were, they said she was a sure thing. We went on a couple of dates, and by date four, I was ready to go. So Jeff and I concocted a plan. We would take our girlfriends to Jeff's girlfriend's dad's apartment. Her dad, she had told Jeff, was in the midst of a midlife crisis. I imagined Jeff's girlfriend's father in Boca Grande: fishing with a much younger woman with teased blond hair who smoked Marlboro Menthol 100s, having margaritas, pretending to like The B-52's, talking about how his next car would be a Mazda RX-7.

Anyway, the point was that his apartment, just like his soul, was empty and literally right around the corner from where we lived, and even closer to the only spot in North Tampa where we knew we could get alcohol. So we got a case of Natural Light and rented *Pet Sematary* (figuring at the very least, we'd scare the girls onto our dicks). We bought two condoms from a gas station bathroom (conservative) and as we pulled up to the apartment, shit was on.

The Saint and I sat through roughly twenty-five minutes of *Pet Sematary* before I suggested we retreat to Jeff's girlfriend's makeshift hey-this-is-your-condo-too bedroom.

The rest was a car wreck. I'll do my best not to leave out any details.

I laid her on the bed and in a matter of seconds I'd undressed her like she was covered in ticks. I still had all my clothes on—baseball hat, jacket, jeans, boots. I dropped my pants to my ankles and pulled out my condom. This was, it should be noted, the first time I'd ever tried to put on a condom, a feat I wish now I had practiced. Young men don't often buy condoms and try them on in their rooms, just to see how they look, although maybe they should give it a try. I was too embarrassed at that point to buy condoms at a grocery store. Hence our stealthy purchase at the vending machine inside a gas station's dirty bathroom.

I unwrapped the condom only to find, much to my surprise, that it was rolled up like a sock. I don't know what I was expecting—maybe a fourfold? But my mom still did my laundry, so I said to myself, "This must be rolled up the way my mom rolls up my socks." So I began *unrolling* the condom in my hands. When it reached a length that seemed suitable for someone with a great jump-shot, I stopped, then rolled it back up to a more reasonable, qualified-for-a-home-loan penis-sized length. Then I took the unsleeved condom, put it at the explosive end of my junk, and pulled it down. One problem, there was air trapped between my dick and the end of the condom, so as I pushed down, the condom inflated. I tried three or four times before I realized I was making balloon animals on my dick. Meanwhile, The Saint patiently waited for me to begin banging guts. I tried to squeeze the air out of the condom, but this only made things worse, more hilarious balloon animals. At first a giraffe, then a lion, always returning to a manatee. After a few futile attempts I realized this was a no-go. I stood and pulled my pants back up, walked out the door into the living room, and approached Jeff. I told him I needed to speak to him in private.

I took him into the kitchen, cracked another Natty Light, and told him my dilemma.

"I need the other condom."

"You're done already?"

"Long story."

"You can't be done already?"

"No, it was broken."

"How was it broken?"

"Does it fucking matter? The gas station must have fucked it up; give me the other fucking condom, please."

"But what am I gonna use?"

"Look, I have her naked in the other room and shit is going down as soon as I get back in there. Be a friend."

A friend till the end, Jeff gave me the cool-guy-condom-handshake, which I now know to be the cool-guy-cocaine-handshake, and I retreated back to the room. I considered phrases like, "pinch the reservoir tip" and "unroll onto the shaft." The Saint was still lying there, waiting for me. I took a seat, pants at ankles, and then did as instructed. I was ready to go. Putting on the condom even felt kind of good. I took position on top of The Saint, pressing my body against hers, and started.

And finished, almost immediately.

I was like a bull rider, six seconds and I was off. Now all I needed was Hartley to come in dressed as a clown to distract her so I could make a clean getaway from what was sure to be an awkward conversation, because I could tell by the look on her face that she hadn't even begun. But I had no idea how awkward it was about to get. That was when she said seven words no man ever wants to hear.

"Are you going to put it in?"

I may not have the award-winning penis at the fair, but I didn't think I had the sideshow penis. My penis was huge considering my 170-pound frame. Now, on a 240-pound body, it looks odd, like a squatter in the midst of a bustling city. But that is only because I have outgrown it. On my seventeen-year-old body it looked majestic. My confusion turned to panic when I looked down only to find that my dick was wedged between her butt cheeks and the bed.

I hadn't lost my virginity to a person. I lost my virginity to a mattress.

If it's life's biggest moments that define you, then this one defined me as a loser. I didn't think about what to do next, I simply acted. It was my only option. So, even though I was already finished, I stuck it inside her. Truth be told, it wasn't really better than the mattress. I can't say I enjoyed it. But still, I pounded away dutifully, knowing full well that the treaty had already been signed. She did her best to make a show of enjoying it. When I figured she was done, I pretended to be done, too. I walked out of that bedroom and into the bathroom a failed man. I'll never forget looking myself in the mirror that night in the bathroom and shaking my head.

We left that night and I dropped everyone off. As I merged onto the interstate to get back home, I scanned the radio for a song that would put the evening's events in perspective. What I found was Ice T's "Colors." I tried as

I pulled onto the interstate to raise my fist through the sunroof in victory, but the action just didn't fit the feelings. So I drove home in silence, past my curfew, and lied to my parents about the night's events, knowing full well they would prefer it that way.

The Saint and I dated for a couple months after that, before she started sleeping with my buddy Jeff. I didn't need to ask but somehow knew he was much better at sex than I was. I didn't have sex again until college, but by the time I did it again, I had learned some tricks of the trade. Most importantly, masturbate furiously before having sex with a stranger. You've got to unload your gun before you put it in the car to go hunting. Unload it. I did just that—twice—and I lasted so long, I wonder now if she thought I was gay. I ended up dating that girl for five years until she, too, decided to sleep with Jeff. (By now I figured he must be amazing.) And even now, years later, I have shared that awkward moment people call sex—I call humiliation—with only six people.

Seven, if you count mattresses.

4.

I Am The Machine

I grew up in the beauty of the Cold War, when we knew who our enemies were and it wasn't racist to hate them. So, I knew very little about the Soviet Union growing up other than that Russians were cold, unpleasant people who rarely smiled—mostly because their clothes were gray and uncomfortable. Their women had moles and their men drinking problems. They had bad haircuts and were still losing their minds over Jordache jeans while we Americans were outgrowing our Guess. They were our equals athletically only because they were taken from their parents at a young age by a government they hated and fed steroids, while simultaneously killing their retarded. They would cheat on the playing field if they could, because they were evil, but they never cheated in the workplace, which is why they were economically inferior to us. We on the other hand were strong and fashionable. We were fair, honest, openhearted, and loved our "mentally challenged."

I believed all of this wholeheartedly until the wall fell. Then I joined in with the rest of the world in applauding the Russians, like they were a cousin who had finally come out of the closet. In time they would catch up to speed with us, like the rest of the world, but for now they had a lot of growing up to do. And like most Americans, I didn't think of Russia much at all after that—that is, until my (first) junior year of college.

I was living in a tenured teacher's house who had taken a sabbatical after what he called "trumped-up charges of statutory rape, cocaine dealing, and kidnapping" when I accidentally signed up for a Russian language class. I walked into the first session of the noon class sincerely thinking it was Spanish, and the first thing I noticed, the teacher was hot. Smoking hot.

As the other students began to take notes, I closed my eyes in the back of the room hoping to nod off, dreaming that I was living in an apartment in Pamplona above a preschool. That's when I heard the room in unison clearing their throats. I opened my eyes, looked up and noticed the hot teacher was writing a new alphabet on the chalkboard. I leaned over to the kid next to me and whispered, "When did Spanish get a new alphabet?" He chuckled and got back to notes. I leaned in closer and repeated myself more intently. He looked at me a bit confused. "This isn't Spanish, this is Russian."

And with that I was up, like I just noticed an Adam's apple on a first date. *Who the fuck wants to learn a dead language?* I thought to myself. We beat them, they should learn our language, not vice versa. I looked around at the room and saw what I believed to be a bunch of blacksmiths, excited to learn a dead trade, and I was prepared to politely make an exit when the hot teacher stopped me.

"Are you leaving?"

I smiled and explained my mistake to her and the class and got a huge laugh. Not what I was looking for, but I took it and excused myself.

Before I could get out the door, she cut me off and kindly asked if I would stay. I usually didn't even sit in on classes I was enrolled in, let alone ones I planned on dropping, so her request challenged my hard-earned slacker value system. But her wholesome looks and Midwestern charm prevailed, and so I decided to stay for just that one class.

At the end, she pulled me aside and explained her conundrum: Without me, they didn't have the minimum number of students required to keep the class going. It would have to be canceled. The students who wanted to take Russian wouldn't be able to. She told me if I decided to stay onboard, she guaranteed that I would get no less than a C.

A shocking offer, I'm sure, to anyone that attended a serious four-year university. But this was FSU and while I can't speak for everyone, this was not the first proposition of the kind I'd received. Regardless, it was an interesting orgy of feelings to have fornicating in my head. For a second, I remembered my uncle telling me that Russia after the wall would be like the Wild West. Americans with a subtle knowledge of the fundamentals of business would be able to swing over there, open up McDonald's and ATMs and make millions. I had at best that subtle knowledge, and what better way to make my millions than by conquering a foreign land. And I presumably would have had to *attend* and *sleep through* the Spanish class I had planned on *attending* and *sleeping through*—so I sat in on her Russian 1 class just enough to hold up my end of the bargain, and at the end of the semester I got my C.

The next semester, we all signed up for Russian 2 with the exact same teacher, and guess who got another C? Why not? I had taken Russian 1; it seemed like the reasonable thing to do. There were a number of times she tried to get me to really focus—to show me what I was missing by not taking her class seriously. But I would always retreat from what seemed like the insurmountable task of learning, and I was perfectly comfortable cruising through and getting my C's. I'm not proud of it in hindsight, especially as a father of two daughters who I hope will take advantage of all that college has to offer (except, obviously, for the designer drugs and virginity-saving anal sex). But I was twenty-two and had just discovered mushrooms and disc golf. Academics weren't my first priority.

By the end of Russian 4, she was teaching the entire class in Russian, and I was sitting in attendance feeling lost, like an immigrant at the DMV. All my dreams at that time were in Russian, which made dreaming especially terrifying, because I didn't speak the language any better than I did four semesters earlier. Russian men constantly shouting at me while I shouted back, "I don't know what you are saying!" I figured my happy hour of guaranteed C's was reaching last call, when our beautiful teacher asked if we wanted to go to Russia to study abroad and get a minor.

Get a minor was a tad bit misleading. After a few awkward conversations with some classmates, I realized she was speaking academically. I hadn't even declared a major, and here I was with the prospect of getting a minor in a language I couldn't even speak, read, or write. It sounded too good to be true.

When I attended the mandatory informational meeting for the study abroad program, I locked eyes with my teacher, one of four adults presiding over the meeting, and saw a shocked look on her face, like that of an adulterer confronted at church. Afterward, she pulled me aside.

"What are you doing here?"

"Going to Russia?"

"This is for serious Russian language students."

"I'm taking Russian 4," I reminded her.

"Bert, we both know you can't speak Russian."

"So I can't go?"

"Are you serious?"

"Honestly, I told my dad about it and he really wants me to go." (This was true. My dad will shock you at times with what he green-lights: speed, edible marijuana, and Russia to name a few.)

"I'll have to talk to the head of the Russian Department."

I nodded. What did I have to lose?

A week later after class, she asked me to come with her to her office. She sat me down and a man I had never met before sat across from me. He looked like the Marlboro man. He was tall, with blond hair, and had the air of a secret agent. He was the kind of guy you meet and automatically assume has a fat cock and knows how to use it. (Hopefully that's not just me.) Just like in a spy thriller, he whispered something to me in what I was now familiar enough with to know was Russian. After four semesters of the language, I may not have been able to speak it, but

I was definitely proficient in knowing when other people were. I smiled and nodded, darting my eyes from my teacher to the man and back to my teacher. He said it again only to receive the same blank stare, like I was waiting for my pupils to fall from my eyes. He looked at my teacher and shook his head.

"You weren't kidding, he really can't speak a word of Russian."

"I told you so," said my teacher.

The man, who I would later learn was the head of the Russian Department, leaned across the table and made me a blunt offer. "You can go, but you have to promise to *never* take another Russian class ever again."

I considered his offer, looked at my teacher, smiled, and said, "Deal."

A few months later, we were on a plane headed to the motherland. I was in the back with an open seat next to me, drinking heavily and fantasizing, as most men do, about all the sex and possibilities that lay ahead of me the second we touched down. The girl in the sundress on a bike that I'd meet on the street, the small village she would live in on the outskirts of the city, our nights in her family's onion field, sitting on top of a Yugo watching the stars, falling in love. How her family's neighbors would beg me to stay and become their mayor, how I would end up living there, telling the villagers stories of my exploits as the starting pitcher for the New York Yankees. How I had invented the car wash, explaining what a car wash was, then opening a line of very successful car washes all over the country called Bert's Squirts. We would marry, have children, and spend our summers in the small village where I met her and our winters on the Caspian Sea listening to The Smiths.

I had always assumed my teacher understood me, so when she sat in the seat next to me, in the midst my daydream, in the middle of the night, somewhere over the Atlantic, and asked if she could show me something, my heart started racing. The sex was starting now, I realized as she started unbuttoning her jeans. I almost began drooling, when she did something very unexpected: she pulled out a fanny pack filled with money.

"I'm freaking out about this," she said. "The department gave me ten grand in cash and told me I need to sneak it into Russia."

"For what?"

"The mob."

The mob, I thought. *Why would we have to pay off the Italians to visit Russia?*

As it turns out, the Russian mob had risen up after the fall and had taken over Russia and made it a business to routinely shake down foreigners. A group of our size, from a state school, was as tantalizing as a brand-new pair of

Jordache jeans must have sounded ten years earlier. So the head of our Russian Department (the guy with the fat cock) saw to it that we'd hire two younger mafiosos to chaperone us around St. Petersburg. We offered a good price, and they were going to accommodate by sending two dudes to shadow our every move and make sure that no one laid more than a casual eye on us.

"And that," she said, "is how you do business in Russia."

She had learned about this arrangement at the airport, and she was as nervous about the prospect of having gangsters live with us as she was about having to smuggle their payoff into the country.

My teacher by now was a sort of friend, and I felt empathetic for her plight. I, on the other hand, was bubbling. I had always envied guys like Frank Sinatra, Tupac, Snoop, and Dre. They were artists who were just as comfortable hanging out with entertainers as they were with gangsters. In some parallel universe I fancied myself like them, and now I was going to get a chance to meet actual real-life gangsters. She told me not to tell anyone, went back to her seat, and left me spinning wildly with ideas of what was to come. As I drank myself over the Atlantic, through Prague and into St. Petersburg, I made a resolution: Fuck the dumb chick in the village of morons, I was about to get in real tight with the Russian mafia!

I was too drunk to notice Igor when we deplaned in St. Petersburg. It was only when we checked into our hotel that I realized who he was. The head of the Russian department was there, not only to welcome us to Russia, but to introduce us to our "tour guides," who would be following us around the city. He said they spoke little English and asked us not to engage with, bother, or talk to them. I, on the other hand, had already decided they were going to be my best friends.

I spent the rest of the orientation sizing up Igor. He actually seemed pretty normal, and he smiled more than I thought a gangster should. Igor looked like he might have been beat up a lot as a kid. He was maybe a bit rougher than an American of his age, rocking greasy jet-black hair and a constant cigarette in his mouth. But he definitely wasn't what I expected. He said next to nothing in our meeting, leading me to believe he didn't speak English, and excused himself to his room in the middle of the orientation.

I worried that my opportunity to introduce myself to our "chaperone" was lost, but by the grace of god, his room turned out to be directly next door to mine, across the hall from my hot teacher's.

After orientation, I walked the streets of St. Petersburg, pretending to sightsee, but actually looking for a bottle of nice vodka and a case of beer. Extremely difficult, you can imagine, when your linguistic abilities are equal to that of the average stray canine. My four semesters of Russian were no help, except I was very used to not panicking when people talked directly to me in a foreign language. But eventually I found and overpaid for a cheap bottle of vodka, a six-pack of a beer called Baltika, and stole a lemon.

As the sun set, I grabbed my pocketknife, threw on my fanny pack, and with the nerve of a soldier fighting in a war he believes in, I knocked on Igor's door.

When the door opened, I immediately noticed two things. First, there was a small party happening. This I hadn't expected. I had hoped for a one-on-one with the man, where Igor would be impressed by my gregariousness, generous party favors, and friendly face. Second, there was his "casual" look—cigarette still in mouth, but wearing a wifebeater, track pants, and a most uninviting expression.

He met me with a gruff voice and I knew enough Russian to understand the gist of his muttering.

"What do you want?"

I'm sure he was expecting me to ask them to keep it down. I felt as welcomed as a lump in his nut sack. In a panic, and not really sure how I was supposed to respond, I said the first and only words that came to me in Russian, words that would define me for years to come.

I said, in Russian: "I am the machine."

It was one of the only things I knew how to say after

my four years in the department—that and "I work with cats," which I believed loosely translated to "I work pussy." These were things I would accrue in a moment of attention in class and drop at a party back at school. I was told later that I must have been thinking I was saying, "I am a man," which I'm sure he could have deduced by himself, and sounds now like an extremely direct gay proposition. But regardless of why or how I said it, I said it.

I tried to read Igor's facial expressions, hoping that through them, I could figure out what my words meant. My heart raced and I started to panic until something unexpected happened. Igor cracked a smile. In broken English he asked, "What did you just say?"

Not sure what I had said, but confident that it had made him smile the first time, I repeated it in Russian.

"I am the machine!"

His smile widened. He put his arm around my neck and in even better English than before, said, "Come in and tell my friends what you just say."

Smiling back, I walked in with him to find a smoke-filled room of Russians. He said something to them that I couldn't understand and looked at me, arm still around my neck. "Tell them what you say."

Not sure if I had told him to fuck his mother, or that they could kill me and fuck me like a mother, I put all my confidence in the moment and proudly said in Russian again, "I am the machine."

The room broke out in laughter, and Igor broke into English almost as good as mine. "So you are The Machine. Well, Machine, sit and do a toast for us." I cracked the bottle and pulled out my knife and lemon, thinking I would introduce them to lemon drops. I got an even bigger laugh. "The Machine runs on lemons," someone said laughingly, and the room fell apart. This, much like the rest of the conversation that night, was in Russian. I struggled to follow, but I was certain of one thing: *I was killing.* They took the lemon from me and taught me how to shoot vodka like a Russian. All I said the entire night to them in their language was, "I am the machine."

And so began the legend of The Machine.

I don't remember much from that night—only that Igor spoke English, played the guitar, laughed easily, and that I was The Machine. The Machine lived out of the box, and never said no. Also, The Machine was the funniest guy they had ever met mostly due to the fact that they had never seen any of the movies that I had grown up on, which inherently played to my advantage. Every night that week, under the radar, we smoked, drank, played guitar, and laughed hysterically as I dropped one-liners from *Caddyshack, Fletch,* and *Uncle Buck,* claiming them as my own.

One day, visibly hungover, my hot teacher asked where I had spent the night drinking. I told her. She was as shocked as she was intrigued. When I told her I was doing it again the next night, she asked me to take her, so I obliged. That night, I introduced her to Igor—and to The Machine—and by the end of the next week, *everyone* was partying in Igor's room.

The interesting thing to know about Igor was that he wasn't a hard-core gangbanger. He was a guy misplaced by Russia's failing government. He had been brought up not to dream of becoming famous or a millionaire, but with simple goals like finding a wife, having babies, and living a carefree life, taken care of by the government. Then things went caca. Now, with a new government in place, he and men like him suddenly had to fend for themselves, stand out from the crowd, and make a name for themselves in order to achieve the life that had been guaranteed to them at birth. So Igor did what many men with few options and less hope do: he got involved in il- legal activity. Igor was a good guy—a guy who knew how to read the streets of Russia, who could tell two minutes in advance when a problem was going to happen. One time at a flea market, Igor grabbed me and my buddy John by the arm and told us in Russian, "Let's go." As we walked away, three men jumped out of the car and ruth- lessly beat another man into submission in front of a bookstore, then put a gun in his mouth and began shout- ing. Igor saw it coming, and he wanted no part of it. I, on the other hand, in typical gawker-American fashion, was pissed I hadn't gotten a picture. I told him next time he saw something like that to let us stay. But that was not Igor—his path clearly was the path of least resistance.

I may have been wrong initially about how hard-core a gangster Igor was, but one thing was for certain: The Machine was making a name for himself. I'd meet Igor's friends and he would rejoice in telling them about the outlandish things The Machine had said or done the night before, like the time The Machine had won four straight games of billiards against the house pool shark and begun singing and dancing with his pool cue, swinging it wildly like a ninja-samurai. It didn't matter that I had taken it directly from Tom Cruise's performance in *The Color of Money*, because they had never seen that movie. All they knew was The Machine was spontaneous and improvisational, a wild card who was fun to be around.

Midway through our stay, I was informed that we were taking a trip to Moscow. Great: see the countryside, maybe I'd bump into that girl in the sundress on the bike; she'd love The Machine. But to my chagrin I found out that Igor would not be accompanying us. When I asked Igor why, he said very simply, "One group runs the trains, and a different group runs Moscow. You'll have different escorts for both, but not me." The next day as he walked us to the train, he told me that he had talked to our new escorts and that they were excited to meet me. Before I knew it, I was eye to chest with our two new Russian bandits, Igor and Igor. (I'm assuming when boys were born in communist Russia it was probably best to keep their names in the state-approved comfort zone. All I'm saying is I didn't exactly meet a lot of Millhouses.) In Russian he told them, "Guys this is The Machine, this is the guy I was telling you about. If you give The Machine vodka, you'll have a great time. Take care of him. You'll laugh all the way to Moscow."

They had smiles on their faces, and while they spoke English better than I did Russian, I asked another classmate, a guy we'll call Big John, to hang with us so we could communicate. Despite his size, John was shy and not a big drinker. He was funny, nice, an all-around sweet guy who loved quoting comedians. But even more importantly, his Russian was impeccable and he looked like a defensive lineman.

He looked at me as they told us to follow them. "They said something about wanting us to sit with them on the train, and the bigger of the two keeps looking at you and saying he can't wait to play with The Machine."

We left our friendly Igor and said good-bye to my class as John and I headed to first class, in the front car of the train with our two new Igors. This was like a horrible Richard Grieco movie, I said to John, only in real life.

Their cabin was much nicer than the ones we passed. The ones our classmates were in had two sets of bunk beds with a three-foot-by-seven-foot breezeway between them, while ours was palatial. When we walked in, the first thing we saw was a spread of cheese, meats, bread, and lots of booze. I felt like royalty—and acted the part. There were two couches, a table, a bathroom, and a bed. The best part was that as the train took off, the people who worked on the train, in the know, came back to pay their respects. When the conductor came back to our cabin to introduce himself, John translated.

"He said it would be an honor to have a drink of vodka with The Machine." And then under his breath, "What have you told these people?"

We took our shots, and then the conductor ripped the stripes off the shoulder of his conductor's uniform and handed them to me, "A present for The Machine."

My jaw dropped as the man who was supposed to be driving this moving train—the same man who I just drank vodka with, the man who had defiled his uniform—anticipated my reaction.

I smiled back graciously, thanking him profusely, as he sat with us and stared at me. The whole time I thought two things: (1) who is driving the train?; and (2) these Machine stories might have gotten out of control.

We killed the only bottle of vodka we had before the train was even out of St. Petersburg. Everyone who worked on the train had said hello and either been introduced to The Machine or had already heard stories about The

Machine. Things were falling into place. John and I laughed big laughs as we shared jokes with whoever was in our cabin. This was exactly how I had envisioned it. I was Frank Sinatra, holding court with my gangsters. The entertainer that could turn thugs into puppies. My name had made the rounds with the Russian mob, and I was *the* guy to party with. While John and I were getting buzzed, Igor and Igor seemed to have hollow legs. With no vodka, they started in on a bottle of peach schnapps, offering us swigs straight out of the bottle. When I declined, they smiled. "Then we go to the bar."

I'm an extravagant man. I enjoy the finer things that come with whatever celebrity I have. This, however, was a type of respect and attention I, to this day, have never seen. As the four of us walked to the bar car, we walked as *mobsters*, just like in the movies, and everyone knew it. Doves flew beside us, a breeze blew back our coats to show our holstered guns, we flicked cigarettes behind our back, to set big explosions. And I was the guy out front. It's like when you see a hot chick with an old guy or a fat black dude and you think, "Who *is* he?" We walked into the bar car, and people stared. I strutted like a peacock with a big dick.

In a voice that was loud enough to quiet the room, the bigger of the two Igors said in Russian, "Machine, get bread."

He started to rattle off his list of party rations in Rus-

sian as I walked behind the bar to find them, and it dawned
on me: I understood what he'd said. I was learning, for the
first time in my life. Before I could congratulate myself, the
next order came. "Machine, grab cheese."

I turned to John excitedly. "I know what they are saying! *I can speak Russian!*" A visibly buzzed John smiled
back at me and said in Russian, "Congratulations."

Now, behind the bar, with a loaf of bread in my arm
and looking for cheese, I waited for Big Igor's next order.
"Machine, grab more vodka."

I was giddy as a two-year-old. "I know what you are
saying!"

"Good." He wasn't as impressed as I was. While everyone else had been learning the language through flash
cards and textbooks, here I was picking it up my way, by
joining the mafia.

"What else?" I said proudly. "Give me another one."

"Grab the money."

"What?" I said, smiling.

"Grab the money!"

And suddenly time stood still.

I remember being hunched over, still looking for
cheese. When I looked up, I saw the bartender standing
against the wall, not making eye contact. He was scared.
As I looked around the room, I saw that *everyone* had that
same look. Everyone was scared. Even John.

Before I could argue, John spoke up.

"He said grab the money."

"I don't want to grab the money."

"I think you should just do it."

Standing half erect, I uttered my last word as an innocent man:

"Huh?"

Big Igor was busy going through the pockets of the people in the bar, as he shouted the same command over his shoulder, this time slightly annoyed.

I looked at John. I looked at the bartender. I took the money.

I grabbed a couple bottles of vodka, gave up on the cheese, and we left. As we made our way out of the bar car, I made eye contact with a couple of kids in our class who had seen it all. For a split second I felt cool—cool like the first time you smoked pot, or drank beers in high school. Outlaw cool. As we walked past the coach cabins to our cabin, the cool feeling that comes with committing a felony quickly faded to panic. I was the man behind the bar. I was the one with the bread and the vodka. I was the one who had displayed the spoils of our treachery for all to see.

When we got back to our first-class cabin, things were a little more solemn and the drinking escalated. My teacher came after hearing of our escapades, more to check in than to reprimand us.

I was silently hoping the two Igors would pass out and that I could return to my classmates in coach, but my dreams were dashed by the entrance of a teacher I will simply call SHE. SHE was a substitute chaperone who did not much like me, even before I robbed the train. SHE was in her fifties and fancied me a stupid frat boy, which SHE was mostly right about. SHE opened the door to our cabin and began berating me in front of the two Igors.

"You are done! It's over! You, mister, have a huge lesson to learn in how to be an ambassador for your university and for your country. Stand up right now, the both of you and let's go! Because I—"

Before SHE could finish, Big Igor took a sip of vodka, spit it in her eyes, and said, "No one talks to The Machine like that."

John and I were terrified of what would happen. But SHE was as scared as we were. It was like witnessing a tidal wave firsthand and realizing you are not in as much control as you think you are. SHE said nothing, looked at neither of us, frozen.

Igor shut the door in her face and smiled at both of us. "Fuck that bitch. This is Russia," he nonchalantly said. "When it gets dark, we'll have good time."

To our dismay, the debauchery hadn't even started. Igor and Igor had keys to the entire train and we were about to play Butch Cassidy to those other Sundance Kids. John looked at me in horror as he listened in on their conversation.

"We're robbing everyone," he said with a forced smile.

"Huh?" I said, smiling back.

"I think we are robbing the entire train."

"Really?"

"Really."

And sure enough, as the sun set and conversations subsided to snores, the four of us were off like the Newton Boys.

As we walked out of their cabin, John pulled me aside. "We can't rob the train, but we can't leave them either, or really bad shit might happen to our classmates."

So we accompanied them, forcing vodka down their throats at every opportunity, while the Igors, with our help, robbed our classmates.

I have to say as terrified as I was of the situation, the Igors proved to be the two least insightful thieves I'd ever seen work. Big Igor would unlock the door, not so quietly I might add, while little Igor would crawl on his stomach into the room and go through whatever bags were on the floor. Big Igor would go through their above-floor shit, and if anyone woke up, Big Igor would spit vodka in their faces (now his signature move). Luckily for our class, Igor and Igor were too drunk to do it well. We half-robbed roughly everyone before the rest of our class woke up and we darted off.

The rest of the evening is blurry. I remember John and I decided to continue our attempt to get the Igors as drunk as possible so they'd pass out, which meant getting *ourselves* as drunk as humanly possible in the process. The train was moving fast. I know this because I have a vivid memory of taking turns holding each other by the thighs, hanging halfway out the windows, feeling the cold air punch our faces. We smoked a ton of cigarettes, we took pictures of me taking a shit, and at one point, Igor and Igor left, telling John they had to make their rounds. Not sure what there "rounds" entailed, we rejoiced in our few free minutes of unfiltered conversation. We even went back to our class to make sure no one was hurt, then caught back up with the two Igors to continue our partying in first class.

We approached Moscow as the sun started to come up, and my teacher opened our cabin door. Igor and Igor were semiconscious so she quickly broke the news. The class had been robbed, SHE had been assaulted, and the police had been notified. She explained that they would be waiting for John and me on the platform when we arrived.

After she left, we tried our best to tell Igor and Igor the bad news, only to have them laugh it off. "Deece is fahking Russia!" they said in English. "Fahk police!"

Their reassurance didn't quite have the calming effect it was meant to.

"We *fahk* police in mouth!" All I could do was wonder what kind of trouble they had gotten in while they had been making their rounds—whether we would be held responsible for those crimes, too, or just the felonies we had committed. I prayed that "*Fahk* police in mouth" was a euphemism we weren't familiar with, like "He got his ass handed to him."

My mind spiraled as I imagined my life with John in the gulag. We'd start by being bitches, living in the mud like animals, being owned by older gangsters who had been there since Stalin. We'd get tattoos from tire rubber on our cocks, like good Russian gangster bitches. We would probably date each other on the DL for nostalgia and conversation, while maybe dating stronger men for protection? And that would be just the first year. This was not how I planned on spending my third junior year.

When the train came to a full stop, I opened my eyes hoping to find a passed-out Igor and Igor whom John and I could sneak past, but as fate would have it they were just starting that day's drinking, smoking fresh cigarettes, and laughing loudly. I opened our door and looked out the window onto the train platform where I saw my destiny awaiting. Two cops stood dutifully taking a report from my classmates, most of whom were in their pajamas, some of whom were crying, others somehow still covered in vodka.

I looked back at John, who had his head in his hands,

then at our Russians, whose fate I'd be tied to for the rest of my life. They realized what I was looking at and came to the window only to laugh. Big Igor lit a fresh cigarette, and with a bottle of vodka in hand, headed out of the train onto the platform to offer a counterstatement, one I got the feeling he had *not* been working on.

My class backed away at his arrival. Again, life slowed down. Little Igor walked out of the train and took position next to Big Igor as John and I watched them present their defense, which had more finger-pointing and shouting than I'd have liked.

John looked at me with fright and said, "I think Igor just called his mom a goat. Let's hope that's a compliment in Russia."

Then the finger-pointing took aim at us. It was followed by head shakes, which was followed by shouting, which was followed by more arguing than I was comfortable with, all of it vaguely steered in our direction. The shouting escalated and the cops motioned for John and me to come to them as they barked out some inaudible command in Russian, which, to two kids who grew up watching movies like *Rocky IV* and *Red Dawn*, sounded ominous. As we slowly made our way, the cops began walking to meet us. Their stares never faltered.

I looked at John and said, "I won't say a word, you speak Russian, explain to them clearly what happened, and please get us out of this."

I took a deep breath as we met them. John, in his best I-fucked-up body language, tried to take pole position, only to be shoved off to the side. It was clear: I was to be the patsy. I was Keyser Söze.

I tensed as one of the two cops grabbed me by the arm and pulled me to the side. It was a moment of clarity—one when you know your life is about to change forever, when your asshole gets ice cold and you realize just how much you fucked up a great life. It's the moment they find the pound of coke in your suitcase, or the hash taped to your body, or the tumor in your brain. Life as you knew it will always be a depressing memory. That was then, this is now.

They waited for what seemed like an eternity, then all of a sudden the smaller of the two cops cleared his throat and leaned in toward me.

He whispered, "So I understand you are The Machine?"

I said nothing. I nodded gently. I looked over to Igor and Igor, who were too busy making fun of my class to notice us. I looked at John, who looked back for a hint of what was going on, when the taller of the two cops started laughing.

"Tonight," he said, "you party with us."

I leaned in and gently whispered, "We are not in trouble?"

He looked over his shoulder, then back to me, and whispered back, "No, fuck that bitch, this is Russia!"

Things happen on trains, he told me, and he mentioned also that he had my hotel information and would call us later that night. John and I got on a bus with a class full of people who hated us and spent the rest of the day touring the Kremlin, as hungover as Yeltsin must have been the day after his inauguration.

I would like to say that I got into some hijinks that night with the two cops, just like I had on the train. That I have an awesome story about driving their cop car around after going to a strip club with their friend who was a plastic surgeon, and shooting machine guns in a forest, contemplating the possibilities of doing the same only while getting a blow job. To be honest with you, if I had known that night I would still be telling this story at forty years old, I might have killed a man.

But it didn't happen that way. That night John and I lay in our beds in a room we were sharing and simply listened to the phone ring, over and over and over.

5.

Givin' Out Spankin's

No matter how successful I may get, I'll always be a failed musician, sitting at a concert double fisting overpriced twenty-ounce beers, wishing it was me on stage brooding soulfully to my fans. I had my shot once, but I let it slip through my fingers like cocaine on a roller coaster. I'm sure that ultimately I would never have been taken seriously as a musician. The low-rise leather pants never fit, and they still don't. (Turns outs a size 40 in leathers is a bit pricey—lots of cows.) But to know that rock stardom was within reach, and I let it go, will always loom over my head.

I learned to play guitar a couple months after losing my virginity in eleventh grade. My dad bought me a Martin acoustic and my childhood friend John Noonan, who was now king of the alt scene at our high school, taught me how to play "She Talks to Angels." I was hooked. Every day we'd hang out at lunch in the yearbook room, and he and his friends would show me the basics of the guitar and debate who was better, Siouxsie and the Banshees or The Cure, all while subtly inspiring me to grow my hair out. My repertoire started to grow from there. "Every Rose Has Its Thorn" (a panty-dropper at the time), "Brown-Eyed Girl," "Wish You Were Here"—Base Camp for every high-school kid who at one point planned on summiting the peaks of college pussy. I was always funny, but the soft sensitive musician was a new hat for me and I liked the shade it gave my face. I graduated high school, and my guitar and I moved to Tallahassee. I was still a hack, even then, but like Dirk Diggler's dick, I'd whip it out at parties, bonfires, any chance I had to impress girls.

It wasn't until my second sophomore year that things got serious. I was at a fraternity party, playing the same set of songs, when two of my fraternity brothers, Ben Carter and John Dacre, approached me with an idea.

"I have a garage, Ben has a drum set. I say we teach Brackin [John's roommate and best friend, Brent Brackin] how to play bass and start a band."

"What will I play?"

"I'm a better guitar player than you, so we think you should be our front man."

My ego exploded as I put imagery to the sentence:

Me, shirtless, in shape, bottle of whiskey for breakfast, girls listening to my every word, tour buses, a house in Jamaica. I grow a beard, I write a book, I go back on tour, me shirtless again, back in shape, getting led offstage by police, girls screaming, whiskey, cocaine, a hotel room, a Haitian model, room service, grandchildren . . .

"We'll learn a few songs, get booked at bars, get free beer."

In a town like Tallahassee, your partying defines you, and the idea of being a band's front man—standing on a stage in front of thousands of my peers, leading the night in song, downing as many free beers as I could manage—seemed like a dream. It was more than enough reason for me to say yes. I was sold.

For the first time in my life I started doing my homework. It was easy, I wanted to be a front man. So I'd listen to songs that my bandmates could play, memorize the words, learn how to sing them. I did my homework dutifully. Or at least I did at first. Every night I'd sit in my room with a case of beer and a pack of cigarettes, listening to a batch of songs. But I found out very quickly that the *idea* of becoming The Front Man was actually more important to me than minor details like learning lyrics or better yet, learning how to sing. I started to spend less time practicing the songs and more time watching movies like *The*

Doors. I was enthralled with the idea of creating a character like Jim Morrison. At the time, Nirvana had just taped their *Unplugged* album, and John gave me a video of the performance. Candles, cardigans, greasy long hair covering Kurt Cobain's face, I found myself practicing his small nuances more than his lyrics. Don't get me wrong, the music was great, some of the best ever. But Kurt in the sweater, awkward, fumbling, and distracted—to me, that's what made the performance. It was the same with The Doors. I loved their music, but the idea that Jim Morrison would hang out of hotel windows hammered on drugs and alcohol—for some reason, it made the music that much richer.

It became my mission. Get large, get loud, and get living. I started by putting a keg in Dacre's garage where we practiced. *Who sang sober?* Singing was like sex: vulnerable, revealing, and done better drunk and in the dark, I thought. I adopted quirks: I would only drink Mountain Dew and eat Cheetos. This would really pay off when we put it on the rider for our first stadium tour. Next were clothes: Doc Martens, jeans, beat-up T-shirts, and cardigans would be my uniform. And lastly, outlandish behavior. I adopted a motto: Never say no. Jim Morrison never said no, Kurt Cobain never said no. You couldn't have great things to write about if all you did was sit in your living room with your roommates talking about the phone bill. I needed to get out there and start living. I read Hunter S.

Thompson for the first time, smoked weed, went on walks in the woods, climbed to the roof of our house and sang to the moon. How could I consider myself on a path to front-man greatness if I turned down opportunity? (More than the quirks or the clothes, this motto sadly has carried on into my adult life.)

I started living the life. Getting naked in public became the norm, taunting police while hanging, Gene Autry style, off of a light post on Tennessee Street was a typical Monday night. Practicing music, however, was not on my list of things to do, and it showed at our first band practice. Our bassist, Brackin, was new to the instrument, and much to our chagrin, he had been practicing the bass as much as I had been practicing my vocals, which is to say not at all. This, coupled with the fact that we had a fresh keg of beer at the ready, made getting through an entire song impossible. Not to be dissuaded we convinced ourselves that no band starts off sounding like The Beatles, not even The Beatles. So we let our two good musicians, Ben and Dacre, jam while Brackin and I got drunk and watched.

This is how our first month of band practices proceeded. We would all meet in Dacre's garage and struggle to get through a Nine Inch Nails song until Brackin and I gave up. We drank and John and Ben jammed on. Until one day everything clicked. For the first time, after being together for a mere month and a half, we actually played an entire song together. We were so pumped that we played it again, even better, and again, maybe this time a little worse. On our third time through the same song, I lost my voice. We laughed it off, high on our own praise. It was just a fluke. We proceeded to put aside our instruments and get down to killing beers.

The next day at band practice we realized two things: (1) it was not a fluke; and (2) when I did have a voice, I more often than not sang the wrong lyrics. Ben kept interrupting run-throughs of our one song, "Wish," by Nine Inch Nails. He would simply stop drumming and yell, "What the fuck are you saying?" I would tell him I was only singing the lyrics that ol' Trent had written. Ben would inform me that the phrase "pony ride to Applebee's" was not in the lyrics. I would get defensive and tell him that I was being interpretive, putting my own spin on the song. Why could they improvise and make it sound their own while I was forced to sing the *exact* words of the song?

"That's the point of a fucking cover band—to sing songs people know so they can sing along. What you are doing is like Weird Al, but not funny."

"We aren't going to be a cover band for long, anyway, Ben!" I reminded. "Wish" and the other songs were just stepping-stones until we came up with our own material.

And those songs are what we focused on for our second and third month as a band. They'd start playing and I'd go back to butchering lyrics at the top of my lungs.

Beer flowed freely, and it was only a matter of time before everyone was drunk and our rhythm was so far off that we would have to call it a day.

By the end of three months, we had three songs firmly under our belt. "Wish," Jane's Addiction's "Mountain Song," and Nirvana's "Smells Like Teen Spirit." But I was already mentally scrapping these songs, to be replaced with the new material I was writing in my spare time.

In the months of drinking, eating Cheetos, and saying yes, I discovered my sensitive side. I had started reading poetry, Maya Angelou to be specific. Odd I'm sure that a twenty-one-year-old frat boy was connecting with an old black woman, but I liked it. That cleared the path for me to begin writing poetry, which lent itself fairly easily to songwriting. All of this was even better fuel for sitting by myself in my room drinking.

The first and last song I ever wrote was a ballad I was quite proud of, and one I would play for anyone, anywhere. My buddies would see me come into a crowded room and all clamor for a good seat, begging me to play my new song for all the people who hadn't heard it yet. I would nod knowingly, like a celebrity obliging the paparazzi. I'd grab my guitar, improv some riffs and some lyrics, and slide gently into my ballad. What I didn't know was that my friends were only asking to hear it so they could laugh at me behind my back. It was a ballad about date rape called "Mary Margaret" (I'm getting douche chills right now just thinking about it), and to say it gently borrowed its chord structure from the Indigo Girls' "Closer To Fine" would be an understatement. I'll never forget the look on my bandmates' faces when I played it for them for the first time. It is the same look, interestingly enough, that a person gives when they walk in on someone masturbating, only fixed and prolonged.

"Look, this song may not sell a million records, but I got a ton more like it just swimming inside of me and we need to get them out of there and see which ones rise to the surface."

Brackin was the only one on board, mainly because my song asked very little of him as a bassist. Ben and Dacre did their best to go along with it, and within a week we had *four* songs in our repertoire.

That is when they invited *him* into the band.

He was a fraternity brother of ours but a transfer from South Florida. He had gotten into a conversation at the house about wanting to start a band, and they sent him our way. He was a guitar player and had a bunch of equipment, so Ben and Dacre loved him immediately (we were all playing off cheap amps at the time).

The next thing you know *he* was in our band.

His name was Mark and he was actually a really nice guy. The only problem was this: He was an awesome musician, and the equipment he brought into the garage dwarfed ours. As it stood now, you could be in our band

and suck, but he raised the bar so high that when you sucked around him, it became painfully clear. It was like John and Ben had found a porn star to bring to prom, and Brackin and I were their original, ordinary dates. We felt left behind, ignored, fat. Mark, John, and Ben would just start jamming, leaving us no other choice but to start drinking. And, of course, to paraphrase Trent Reznor, therein starts the downward spiral.

The worst part was that as much as Brackin and I hated losing control of our band, drinking beers and listening to three guys shred was actually really fun. One day, I walked into the garage to them playing a beast of a song. A hit for sure. A song that the second I heard it, I knew it would sell a million records. They were so good and so natural, playing off each other like a Brazilian soccer team, that I stopped Brackin from trying to keep up on the bass and poured us both beers so we could sit and listen. When they finished I applauded them.

"Did you guys just come up with that?"

Ben looked to the two guitarists. "Uh, yeah."

"That was amazing! If we put lyrics to it, I seriously believe it could be a hit!"

Dacre leaned in. "You think you could throw some lyrics in there?"

They were all smiles.

"Definitely!"

"Well, let's get it up on its feet," said Ben.

And so I let them play as I hit Record on a tape player close by and started improvising lyrics into my mic. It was going so smoothly that by the time they just randomly started playing a third jam, I started to see a golden light at the end of the tunnel. Dacre and Ben, with Mark's help, could make amazing music that literally wrote itself. The music was catchy, hard-hitting, and original. My lyrics could use improvement, sure. But we were onto something. Maybe—and I knew this was sacrilege—if we got rid of Brackin and got a real bassist we could make a run for it. Bars at first, then clubs, small theaters, arenas. I'd solo, rejoin the band, do a reunion tour . . .

"Guys, these are groundbreaking songs. If you give me a little time to work on the lyrics, we could have some real hits on our hands."

Ben clued me in to what the others already knew: that they had been playing U2 songs. As soon as this came out, the room fell apart laughing. Apparently the only thing more fun than jamming to U2 songs was watching someone try to improve upon Bono's lyrics.

As Mark laughed along, I looked at Brackin. Mere seconds ago I would have told you that our bond as a group was unbreakable. But Brackin knew exactly what I knew: He could have been the one they were mocking. Our connection to the group was fading.

We had to get Mark out of the band.

He was too good. He made our bandmates realize

exactly how much we sucked. Our suckery now shined down on them. They were doing U2 covers for now, but they would get better, and it was just a matter of time until they'd need a new front man and a bassist.

Mark's playing may have been awesome, but not as awesome as our desire to keep our band together. His death came slow, like a deer trapped in a sulfur pit. At first Brackin just stopped telling him when band practice was. Then Brackin and I would sit in the garage and shrug our shoulders at his absences. "Can you believe this guy?" On days when his profound desire to jam drove him to the garage regardless and he'd find us all there, he'd say nothing and just pick up jamming with Ben and Dacre, leaving Brackin and me to simply drink.

Eventually it was a combination of our lack of commitment, and Brackin and my visible antagonism that drove him away. "You might want to take your stuff out of the garage," Dacre finally said to him, joining Brackin and me in the fight after we had a not-so-subtle conversation with him about something Mark may or may not have said. Brackin and I saw this as a victory: Dacre taking our side.

I think Mark was more stunned than anything. His parting words were not of anger but of disbelief. "Seriously? I'm the best guy in the fucking band." He was right, of course. But he left, we stayed together, and he was now the best guy *not* in the fucking band. His exit made us even closer, and we finally settled on a name: Givin' Out Spankin's.

Mark had apparently told some of our fraternity brothers that our band sucked (something I'm sure they already knew after listening to a couple of my impromptu coffee shop–styled performances) and that his band would blow our band out of the water. His band, we were told, was actually pretty good, and had already, within a short period of time, booked a gig. But it didn't matter to us. Despite the fact that we were back down to three songs, we were closer as bandmates than we had ever been. So we all decided to go in solidarity to see them play and size up the competition. They played at a restaurant called the Mill. Pedestrian in my opinion, the Mill was better known for their unbreakable muffins than for breaking bands.

That night, the guys set up their equipment in the middle of the floor, rookie mistake in my opinion. I would have picked a corner to face. That I could play shy to. We took a table in the back with a pitcher of beer, by this time the bloodline of our band, and we waited.

They took the stage and I'll never forget the reaction. Dacre and Ben were impressed, which made Brackin and me only more sure that we had made the right decision. Before the set ended, we made a hasty exit out the back so Mark and his band couldn't see that we'd been there. We mocked them for the entire ride home, laughing hysterically at almost all their decisions. It was as if their front man had done no research on front-manning and only learned how to sing. Mark didn't throw his guitar in the air, and their covers sounded like originals. But as Brackin and I laughed, we could see it in Ben's eyes: We were a dead band walking. As much as we mocked them, they were just too good. All the stuff we laughed at were the things that made them better than us.

As the guys dropped me off you could see the beginning of the end.

"What time is band practice tomorrow?"

"We'll call you."

We tried our best to keep our band together, but within a few months, Mark's band was playing all the bars in Tallahassee, drinking all the free beer I thought would be mine. Eventually, we had no choice but to call it quits. And that was the last time I ever flirted with music.

A couple years later, I ran into Mark and some of his bandmates at a grocery store in Tallahassee, just as I was planning my move to New York. They were off to Gainesville, or Atlanta, or following some other trail that Sister Hazel had blazed before them. I wished them luck and they wished me the same.

I walked away from them that day and said to myself, out loud, "I doubt anyone will ever hear of that stupid band Creed."

Years later, I was hosting *The X Show* on FX. In the meantime, Scott Stapp had stepped in to fill the role I'd once dreamed of. He was the front man to Mark Tremonti's guitarist. *He* was the Jim Morrison I was destined to be.

I reached out to their manager, Smitty, a guy who I had gotten fucked up with a lot back in the day. I asked if we could get Mark on the show. I told him we could talk about what a fool I had been, drink a beer. I'd even play one of my originals, so everyone could have a good laugh. Mark passed. I was surprised but brushed it off. Another time I was driving down La Brea in Hollywood and noticed that the truck next to me was identical to my truck, a black Expedition. I looked closer and realized it was Mark and Scott. I waved wildly to get their attention but they ignored me and drove off. I was shocked but tried to understand. Even more recently, my buddy Cowhead, who has the number one radio show in Tampa Bay, ran into Mark at a party and, having heard this story a million times, asked him if he remembers any of it. Mark said no.

When Ben, John, Brackin, and I bring up Creed now, we laugh off our massive mistake—and their huge success. We've let go of our failures. And actually, I would like to tell Mark publicly, here and now, that if you're still hung up on being forced out of Givin' Out Spankin's, please don't be upset. We're ready to take you back.

6.

American Transit

Eddie Fernandez is the funniest man I know, and I know the funniest men in the world. He's not the kind of witty, smarmy, clever funny that puts hipsters over, not the kind of ironic funny that references obscure pop-culture figures. No, he's the kind that would make a group of Navy SEALS spit beer out of their nose. He is the kind of unbelievable funny that guys love to tell other guys about and often duplicate. His jokes are usually meant for only the people he is with and his ability to keep you laughing is uncanny.

A lot of people might find his sense of humor childish, lowbrow, and inappropriate. Some people, my wife included, might argue that he's not funny at all, that he's bipolar, sociopathic, and outright offensive. And she'd be right—all except for the not-funny part. Those are the things that make him funny. Of course she met Eddie moments after he got a hand job behind a dumpster from a deaf girl he had met at an all-midget KISS cover band concert. I thought his recounting of the event was absolutely hysterical. My wife didn't. I find all of his sexual conquests hilarious and have thought at times that he was only going through with them for my benefit. I can say unequivocally that one thing Eddie likes more than anything is to make *me* laugh.

There was the time, for instance, that I was Eddie's unwitting accomplice when he "mock-kidnapped" a couple of very drunk sorority girls, who had the nerve to push their way into his car. Annoyed, and thinking I would find it hilarious, Eddie decided to take them on a ride they would never forget. They told Eddie to "get them high," and rather than telling them to get the fuck out of his car, Eddie offered to oblige. He drove fast on back roads and quickly had them disoriented, and when they got mad, he started laughing. I started laughing, too, as I was the most confused person in the car. I knew Eddie didn't have weed, didn't smoke weed, and didn't even know where to find weed. So when one of the girls demanded that Eddie turn his car around and take them back to the party immediately and Eddie told her she was in no position to make any demands, my confusion turned to fear. She replied with a threat of screaming, which made Eddie laugh hysterically.

"Scream as loud as you want, no one's gonna hear you!"

I was shocked and made the mistake of saying Eddie's name. Eddie started yelling at me to "Stop saying our *fucking names* or we'll have to kill them." I was just as scared as they were at the time. But I later saw it for what it was: Eddie's attempt to teach a couple of dumb girls a lesson about manners and safety while getting his own brand of retribution. A joke, in short, though someone else might see it as a felony.

Eddie is an amazing judge of character and even better at finding the common denominator that unites people. And if what he sees bothers him, he levies justice—he's a sort of cosmic con artist. One of his favorite things to do was walk up to arrogant hot girls in Hollywood and ask for their autographs. When they obliged, he'd look at them and ask, "Are you famous?" When they'd admit that they weren't, he'd look back at them in disgust, throw the autograph at their feet, and say, "Then get over yourself. You're not better than anyone in here."

His prank calls were legendary, but not in a Jerky Boys way. In college, he would call a number at random out of a sorority directory, with upwards of ten of us listening in. He would answer the girl's hello with "Hey, guess who it is?" Eddie would then be whomever they guessed it was and proceed to wheedle history, back story, and secrets out of the girl. By the end of the call, we'd be amazed at all the information he had mined out of his mark—who slept around, who her roommates were sleeping with, who *she* was sleeping with, who had STDs, who had drug problems. This skill proved unfortunate when he accidentally called one of his girlfriend's best friends and learned that his girlfriend was sleeping with the star point guard for the FSU basketball team. Eddie was devastated. He decided to graduate early and move to L.A. to make it big, to prove to his cheating ex what a horrible decision she'd made.

Eddie was in L.A. both of my senior years at Florida State, and he was one of the first people I called after the *Rolling Stone* article came out. Oliver Stone's company had optioned the rights to my life, I told Eddie, and I had my sights set on stardom. I wanted to live in New York, and I thought Eddie would be the perfect person to have there with me.

Eddie took a long pause after I proposed it. "I hadn't really thought about it. But if you're serious, I'll sell all my shit out here and be there in a month." I wasn't too surprised to hear him say yes. Eddie loved chaos. And just like that, he walked out on his roommate and sold everything he owned.

We would be moving to New York as a team, and I couldn't have been happier.

I moved to New York before Eddie, without a place to

stay. But I still had fantastic social skills, so I came up with a plan. As night fell, I would head out to bars with a big bag of weed and seek out some dudes who looked like me. We'd have some beers, and I'd make them laugh and help them hit on chicks. (State-school kids are leaps and bounds more socially adept than private-school kids.) Then, as the night drew to an end, I would ask them if they wanted to get high. When they said yes, I would tell them that my roommate was a dick and had to be up early, so we should probably get high at their place.

I would plop down on the couch, take a couple hits, and pass the fuck out. Unable to move me, and stoned themselves, they would leave me be. In the morning I would get up, apologize profusely, tell them we should meet up again, and make my exit.

What can I say, it was an ingenius plan and it worked like a dream. I had been doing this successfully for about a week. Then one morning, after a night of smoking pot with this one dude, listening to Tool, hearing him talk extensively about how *My So-Called Life* was the greatest show ever on television, and passing out, I woke to find a guy looking down at me.

"Bert fucking Kreischer?"

Apparently the guy I had conned into letting me crash the night before was living with a high-school friend of mine from Tampa named John Beimer.

After getting over the surprise, John and I had coffee

and I told him everything. It was nice to see a familiar face—someone I could trust and didn't have to put on a front for. He had answers to all my problems.

"As far as a place to sleep," he said, "you can crash on our couch until you find a place or until you get tired of hearing about *My So-Called Life*. And if you're serious about this comedy thing, I can get you on stage next Monday. I'm doing an open mic at the Boston Comedy Club."

John Beimer is the reason I'm working today.

I learned from Beimer that Dave Johnson, a friend of ours from Tampa, would be coming into town, and as luck would have it, Eddie's flight was getting in shortly before our set, too.

Eddie arrived, and within minutes of seeing the city and John Beimer's apartment, he decided New York wasn't for him. Everything was expensive and old, and the people seemed to frown on state-school kids like us.

But that didn't mean we couldn't have a good time. We went as a group to the open mic, as Eddie started hatching an exit strategy. John went on before I did—and bombed. Actually, to say that he bombed is a glaring understatement. He got on stage and literally blanked and forgot all his prepared material. It was awkward, uncomfortable, and embarrassing for him. He jumped offstage and then immediately jumped back on stage to a big uncomfortable laugh, then blanked again. He froze for about thirty seconds and said, "Well, I guess that's the end of my comedy career!" Afterward, Eddie, who John had only known for roughly an hour, sat down next to him to console him.

"Well, the upside is it can't get any worse than that."

John, staring off into the void, said, "It can only get worse."

I had better luck with my own set, but after the show, when we went out to celebrate, Eddie stated the obvious.

"We should probably give him some space. I feel bad going back to his place after he bombed that bad."

"Space is a luxury we don't have," I reminded Eddie.

"I talked to Dave. He said we can drive back to the Poconos with him and stay at his place as long as we want. He said he has plenty of room up there."

I looked at John Beimer, who had just had his hopes of becoming a comedian gang-raped. Eddie's plan suddenly didn't sound so bad. So we hopped in Dave's car and left the city.

The Pocono Mountains were the antithesis of the city. Lush, clean, full of vegetation, it was kind of like being back in a college town, and Eddie loved it. We spent the next two weeks in Dave's mountain cabin with his huge group of friends. While he and his friends were busy working, Eddie and I would drink, eat laxatives, watch *Jerry Springer*, take hikes, and talk about Andy Kaufman.

With no worry of having to find a place to sleep, I was genuinely relaxing for the first time since my move to New York. It was a blast. At night we would hang out with Dave and his friends at the local bar—drinking, laughing, telling stories. For extra money, Eddie and I would post up at the pool table upstairs and run an old fraternity-house pool scam. Super simple: We'd set up a ball in each pocket and they'd have to run the table without missing a shot. They'd pay five dollars to play and would win thirty-five dollars if they could clear the table flawlessly. It looks easier than it is. So by the end of the week we had a pocket full of money (and fewer friends).

But I still didn't have a home to go back to in New York. So when my cousin Abe from Philadelphia called and offered Eddie and me not just a place to stay but two free tickets to see Dave Matthews, we were sold. We decided to hop a bus to Philly the next day.

Eddie was trying to make it as an actor, but he didn't have a lot of work lined up at the time. He had no stage to practice his trade. So he took it upon himself to "workshop" his craft every now and then. A workshop for Eddie usually consisted of approaching a stranger and lying to them until he got caught (which *never* happened). This was his way of keeping up his acting chops. His usual suspects were girls—moderately attractive, maybe a little overweight, and excited to be chatted up by a good-looking, confident Latin man. A Yankees baseball cap would lead to a story about rehabbing a torn shoulder, and the next thing you know, Eddie was the Yankees' newly drafted starting pitcher, taking pictures at the bar with anyone who wanted proof they'd partied with him. Without the Internet access that we all so conveniently now carry in our pockets, these workshops could go on for days. They would evolve and get more elaborate. The next day he was not the rehabbing Yankees' starter they met yesterday, but that guy's twin brother, Mario, who'd opted to go to college and play ball at FSU. It was in good fun for the most part, and these workshops usually ended with everyone laughing about the hijinks that had ensued.

Anyway, we left for Philly early in the morning and were in the middle of the long bus ride out of the mountains, still in the foothills, when Eddie leaned forward in his seat, smiled, and suggested we get out and try one of his workshops. Bored from the ride already, I leapt at the opportunity. So we hopped off, threw our bags into a bus locker, and walked into the first bar we found.

It was like every dive bar you've ever been to. Dark, sticky bar to the right, jukebox to the left, and countertop touchscreen video games in the back. We ordered two beers and tried to strike up a conversation with the bartender who, it seemed, was in slow motion, still hungover from the night before. We looked around and realized that all the patrons were older white men, not exactly the talent pool we had been looking for. Had we been interested in advice on how to dodge the Vietnam War and cope with the guilt that followed, this would have been the place. But we weren't, and the fact that it was still arguably morning made drinking beers in a dark depressing place that much less enjoyable. So we finished our first and only round and left, walking back toward the mountains and into a Mexican restaurant. As we opened the doors, Eddie said, "Follow my lead, and remember, the rule of improv is 'Yes and . . .'" It occurred to me: I had always been a by-stander to Eddie's stunts, listening in on a phone line while he spun a web of deceit. Now I was part of the troupe.

We sat down at the bar and within seconds our bar-tender, kind of cute, smiling, walked up to us. Eddie didn't hesitate.

"We need two shots of tequila, two margaritas, and two beers," he barked and turned to me, "because this needs to start happening *now*, and happening more often. Because if this is how it's going to go down, it's going to take us five fucking years, and we need to have it in by the end of the summer or the publishers at MTV are going to have our heads!"

The confused bartender prepared our order, her curi-osity clearly piqued. Eddie kept on. "Seriously when we sold this thing, you said it would happen 'all the time' and here we are, week three, with nothing written. I want you to drink those drinks and make it happen. Either that or go to that table and start writing."

Eddie looked at me for a response as the bartender arrived with our drinks. I realized that in fact *everyone* in the restaurant was staring at me now, waiting for me to say something.

"Sorry."

"You're damn right you're sorry. Now you go over there and start writing about this, whatever 'this' is. . . . Write about the damn bus ride for all I care, just write!"

As I took my drinks to the table, I heard the con start.

"I hate to be nosy," the cute bartender said, "but can I ask what you guys are talking about?"

"Talent," Eddie exhaled, and the bartender laughed along with him. As I sat with my back turned, Eddie laid down his story, peppered with just enough truth to be convincing.

"My buddy over there is the Number One Party Animal in the country, or so says *Rolling Stone*. He sold a book to MTV about partying around the country using only the American transit systems—buses, trains. It's called *American Transit*. This is our third week on the road and nothing has really happened. So we stopped here on our way from the Poconos to Philly in hopes that something really massive goes down, but this is our second bar and so far it's proving a bust."

Eavesdropping from my table, I realized this was my cue to come back to the bar and introduce myself, to corroborate Eddie's story. For the next two hours or so, Eddie and I sat with the bartender. We drank and made her laugh, and I watched as she slowly fell in love with Eddie. I don't think either of us realized what a great foundation we had laid until 5 P.M. when other people started showing up. She leaned across the bar and said, "I know this town doesn't seem like much, but we rage here." Eddie and I both laughed, but she was serious. "Why don't you guys take my car, go back to my house, take naps, and let me prove it to you? I live three blocks from here, super easy to get to. My roommate is gone, so you guys can get some rest, shower, come back, and I promise you a party you'll never forget."

With an offer like that, we had no choice but to accept. So we took her keys, found her house, and, as we both lay in her bed, laughed at just how far Eddie's con had gotten us.

"What the fuck is wrong with people that they trust that easily?" Eddie said.

"What the fuck is wrong with you that you can so easily get people to do things like give you their car and house without suspicion."

We giggled, drunk, and fell asleep. When we awoke, it didn't seem so funny. It was dark, we were already hungover, and a stranger had entrusted us with her house and her car. Things had gone too far already and we felt like fucking creeps. We decided that, whatever we had gotten ourselves into, we needed to get out. We would drive back to the Mexican restaurant, give the bartender her keys back, walk back down to the bus station, get our bags, and hop on a late bus to Philly.

But as we pulled up to the Mexican restaurant we noticed that the once empty parking lot was packed. We walked through the front door, heads hung low, to find what I can honestly describe as the hardest raging party we had seen since our days at FSU. Chicks were dancing on the bar, dudes pumping their fists, a python hanging from the rafters (not really, but it felt like that), all while music throbbed out of the sound system.

The party stopped on a dime at our arrival. Then, as if out of a movie, a Seth Green–looking guy approached, opened the *Rolling Stone* I was profiled in, looked at the pictures, looked at me, looked back at the pictures, and then yelled into the crowd, "It's really him!" Again, as if out of a movie, the crowd began to jump, shout, and cheer. I looked at Eddie, who looked back at me in disbelief as we were pushed to the bar where shots were lined up. The crowd was already chanting "Drink" as we approached.

There, we found our hostess smiling. "I called all my friends and told them we had to show you guys how hard we party. I also bought the Tyson fight. Everyone is here for you guys and the drinks are free, so have a good time."

Like any great night of drinking, we were pulled in a hundred different directions, barely hearing anyone, taking lots of shots with strangers, and wondering if anyone would let us put fingers in them. I remember being told how great the Poconos were, how they knew how to party. I remember telling people about *Rolling Stone* and Oliver Stone. And I remember getting into an intense discussion with a guy about how dogs could fuck through a fence and, somehow, how that related to glass blowing.

At the end of the night our hostess gave us a wink as she yelled last call. She pulled us aside and told us to hang back as the bar cleared out, last call didn't apply to us. A moment later I looked over to see a smiling Eddie in front of a table of fifteen girls, at the head of which was our bartender.

Eddie grabbed my arm. "She said they were for us."

This is when things get hazy (also, coincidentally, when the first joint was lit). I remember that the bar was ours to do with as we pleased, and we did. We tried spitting fire. We did belly-button body shots. I set my sights on a tall blonde, who must have told me one hundred times that she "wasn't wearing no panties." We played "I never," and laughed as we walked our way through town and back to our hostess's house, smoking yet another joint.

As we stumbled in, the blonde and I found ourselves on a couch, away from everyone. We kissed the kind of kiss that you can only have with a stranger, the kind of kiss that suggests there is much more to come. I was so high that I literally imagined my hands were Meriwether Lewis and William Clark, exploring recently acquired, unknown territories. They were met with such frenzied excitement to the north that the next logical step for the pair seemed to be to travel south. But as they headed south, they were stopped by Indians. They tried to push forward, but once again, the Indians held their ground. This confused the explorers, considering they had heard so much about the spoils of the land down south.

If you aren't into analogies: I felt her up but she wouldn't let me finger her. I tried one last time so she wouldn't tell her friends I was a quitter when she stopped kissing me and whispered, "Look, I'm just doing enough to get in the book."

So out of it, and sooo wasted, I looked back at her in confusion. "What book?"

"Uh, your book. *American Transit?*"

Right! I did my best to get out of what was now an awkward situation. "Of course, my book, oh you are totally in it."

We went back to kissing, my hands now turning into Frederick Cook and his crew, who explored the terrain of the North Pole. Meanwhile, my South Pole begged for attention.

As this was happening, Eddie, always the gracious guest, figured he owed it to the chick who had set up the entire evening—the bartender whose house we were at—to repay her kindness. He took her back to her room and fucked her.

We left the next morning, thankfully with no fanfare, and caught a bus at the station, sleeping the entire way. That night we recounted the adventure to my cousin and his friends before the concert. And the next day I got a call from John Beimer, who with a heavy heart told me that he was moving home to Florida. If I wanted, I could take his place in New York. So I did. Eddie went back to L.A. to "tie up some loose ends" before moving to New York, and the next month I sublet an apartment on East Eleventh and Third Avenue for the two of us. But Eddie knew from day one that New York wasn't really for him. He lasted half of one month and one Atkins Diet before an opportunity to run some coffee field in San Salvador opened up and he tapped out.

I neither remember the town we stayed in that night, nor do I remember the name of our hostess. I remember the simple layout of the town, that Mike Tyson fought his first fight since getting out of prison that night, and that whatever town that was, they partied harder than most places I've ever been. I sometimes wonder if they remember us, that night, and the stories we told. Who can say?

But I can say this much. Dear tall blonde who wasn't wearing no panties: I don't know what you're doing these days—whether or not you're married and have kids like me, or where you live. I'm genuinely sorry I don't remember your name. But I am a man of my word: You definitely made it into the book.

7.

The Flesh Prince of Bel Air

Now, this is a story all about how my life got flipped, turned upside down, and I'd like to take a minute, just sit right there, I'll tell you about the time I met the Fresh Prince of Bel Air. It was June of 1998 and I had been doing stand-up for roughly six months. My version of stand-up at the time was basically just throwing a party on stage— all crowd work, very little material, even less clothing. This is when *Time Out New York* wrote an article about me, telling the masses that I was their connection to college kids when it came to comedy.

There was some truth to that, but not as much as you'd think. I was younger than most comics working the clubs, having just graduated college a year before, but at twenty-six, I was also well older than the college kids I was apparently connecting with. At the time, I had been working the front door, barking for the Boston Comedy Club in New York City. "Barking" meant that I stood in front of the club and tried to pull any living, breathing person into the club. I basically harassed anyone who dared to walk down West Third Street between Thompson and Sullivan. If I brought in more than twenty people over the course of a night, I got stage time. So, taking into consideration that the club was one block away from NYU, I decided to let any college kid that looked 21-ish into the club for free, often explaining that our drinking-age policy was somewhat lenient. What college kid wasn't going to appreciate the performance of the guy who got him in to see the likes of Dave Chappelle, Dave Attell, Jim Breuer, Jim Norton, Greg Giraldo, Tracy Morgan, Dane Cook, and Jay Mohr for free, and who, with a wink, told him it was a "mandatory" two-drink minimum? In short, I killed in that room.

That, coupled with my reputation as "The Number One Party Animal in the Country" and the piece in *Time Out*, got the eye of a few casting directors—but most importantly it got me noticed by Barry Katz, a talent manager and owner of the Boston Comedy Club. Barry is notorious for two alleged things, rigging *Last Comic Standing* and stealing money from his clients, neither of which happened to me. He read the article and immediately set up a showcase to see me perform. One of the best things about Barry was that he could make magic happen when it came to a young comic's career, mostly because he owned the club you were going to perform at, so he could stack the lineup. Knowing this was my big shot, I filled the room with college kids, ending my set with the story of the time I took acid and went to Disneyland.

Barry liked me and one Friday, he set up another show-case for me to perform in front of David Tochterman, the head of the television department at Overbrook Entertainment, Will Smith's production company. David, Barry told me, had the golden eye when it came to comedy development. He had worked at Carsey-Werner during its heyday and had discovered the majority of their talent: Tim Allen, Brett Butler, Roseanne Barr.

I didn't really have a "tight ten" at the time, so I just improv'd my set. I couldn't tell you what I talked about other than Puerto Ricans and black people; all I know is it was of the moment, and it killed. David approached me after and asked if I would be interested in a development deal. I just melted. Every comic wanted the coveted development deal, the greatest gift you can get from Hollywood, other than a blow job from Scarlett Johansson or seed from Steven Spielberg. A development deal is when a comedian gets paid a ridiculous amount of money not to work for a year—absolutely ridiculous, right?—in order to develop a sitcom for the person paying you. Most of the time they fizzle into nothing, but sometimes they turn into hugely successful TV shows. It was like one attempt at a half-court shot for a million dollars. I had heard about development deals from other comics, but never thought in a million years that I would get one. But there I was, six months into comedy, still working the door at the Boston Comedy Club, with a six-figure development deal hanging over my head.

David and I walked down the street to a wine bar and he explained two things. One, for this deal to go through, Will Smith had to take a liking to me, which was no problem in my opinion since I had been following him since seventh grade. And two, that shaking hands with black men was complicated. After walking me through a parade of handshakes that more mimicked getting tape unstuck from your hand than an actual handshake, he told me that he would set up a meeting with Will for the upcoming weekend and warned me not to fuck up the handshake. I told him I got it.

That Saturday, I was in a taxi with my new manager, Barry, who had staked his claim on my career like a co-dependent pimp, heading to the recording studio that Will was basically living out of while recording his new album, *Willennium*. As we waited in the lobby, I asked Barry to hold my camera and take a picture of us after the meeting. I remember the look on Barry's face when I asked. It was as if I had just told him I'd like him to jerk me off with his feet.

"Papa"—Barry always called me Papa—"you want to be working with this man for the next year, he needs to see you as an equal, and an equal doesn't go into a meeting with an autograph book and a camera. I don't think you should take the picture."

I felt foolish but also thought to myself, *What's the fun of working with celebrities if you don't get a picture to put in your apartment, so when you bring a random chick home from a bar, she gets to look at you in amazement and say, "You know Will Smith? What else do I not know about you? I'm starting to regret my hasty decision not to suck your dick. I think I need to reconsider. . . . Glarg, Glarg."* But I ignored my feelings and agreed, just as the receptionist called me in. We both stood up and she said, "Just him."

Pimp move right out the gate, I thought, as she escorted me down a hallway and into a large dance studio, where two steel folding chairs faced each other in the center.

"Mr. Kreischer, Mr. Smith will be here in a couple minutes. Take a seat."

Mr. Kreischer? I was Bert.

She left me in the middle of the large dance studio surrounded by mirrors. The silence, however, was shortly broken by a hurricane of personality. It was Will Smith, by himself, larger than life, and in fantastic shape looking like Muhammad Ali. Although he had to walk nearly fifty feet to get to me, it seemed as if he made it in three steps. He leaned in and gave me the largest and longest embrace, like we were long-lost brothers.

"One love," he said as we pulled apart. We talked for what felt like a minute but was probably more than an hour, as I babbled on about everything from Tupac, Biggie, Philly, my love of black people, how he was black, how his wife was black, *The Fresh Prince of Bel Air,* how "A Nightmare on My Street" defined him to me. He smiled, laughed, and treated me like an equal, so his request at the end of our conversation didn't seem out of the ordinary to me.

"What are you doing tonight?"

"Nothing."

"You wanna go to the movies?"

"Sure."

"Cool, cool, cool. Meet me at Planet Hollywood at seven."

"Great." I was *stoked.*

"Fantastic. Hey man, this was a great meeting. I can't wait to see you tonight."

"Me, too," I said. He left the room and I headed back out to the lobby to meet my manager, Barry, and told him about our plans for that night.

"Did he invite me?" asked Barry.

"No, just me."

"Wow, that is intimate. Just you and him watching a movie. He must really like you. I didn't even know they had a movie theater at Planet Hollywood."

I hopped in a cab and immediately called my dad, still reeling from my meeting.

"You're going to see a fucking movie at Planet fucking Hollywood?"

"Yeah."

"A celebrity wants you to go to Planet fucking Hollywood with him?"

"Yeah, I guess."

"To see a fucking movie?"

"Yeah. Why does that sound so weird to you?"

"It doesn't sound weird to you?"

I took a moment to think about the proposition.

"Buddy, I think he wants to queer you."

"What?"

"Sounds to me like Will Smith is a Mo-Dicker and he is inviting you to a place so he can get in your pants."

"Seriously, Dad, I think you are way off. I just spent the last hour in a dance studio with him and I didn't get that vibe at all."

"*A dance studio?*"

"Yeah, but it's not how it sounds."

"It sounds like it sounds. Here is what you need to know: most celebrities are closeted homosexuals, that is how they become celebrities, and they find young boys like yourself and 'turn them out.' They call it the casting couch."

"Dad, I think the odds of Will Smith being gay are slim."

"Really? You tell me what is more likely: The fact that you're so talented that six months into being a comedian, the biggest movie star in the world wants to develop a sitcom for you and pay you a ridiculous amount of money and take you out to the movies at Planet Hollywood. Or that Will Smith is gay and wants to fuck you."

He made a convincing argument.

"Oh shit. What do I do?"

"Don't go. Or go, and fuck Will Smith. Here is the deal, buddy: I could be wrong and we'll laugh at this one day, or I could be right. Either way you are never going to know unless you go. I just want to prepare you for the possibility. You know what they say, 'Eat shit, cash checks.'"

As the cab pulled up to my apartment, I saw my roommates walking out of the front door, excited to catch me before they had to go. I hung up with my dad and got out of the cab. I explained how great the meeting was, how everything was beginning to work out for me. But I also started to suspect that I sounded like a Texas prom queen telling her parents how much the Sultan of Brunei was paying her to live at his palace and attend parties.

"That's great!" said my roommates. "What movie theater are you going to?"

"Planet Hollywood."

"They have a movie theater there?"

"I guess."

"Well, you gotta let us know how it goes. Call us the second the movie is out."

I'll call you before that, I thought to myself.

I walked upstairs, starting to debate whether this was a good idea after all. The odds that Will Smith was gay were obviously slim to none, I thought. Since moving to New York, I had developed great gaydar, and he didn't register with me at all. He seemed to me like a run-of-the-mill straight dude. And even though I'd been doing pull-ups every morning, the odds that a regular dude like him was attracted to *a guy like me,* gay or not, were beyond marginal. He saw "something" in me, it was that simple.

But what if it was that he wanted to see something *in me* instead? That very thought ignites a fear so primal in the average straight man that I shuddered. He was a big man, six feet plus, and in great shape, training to be Muhammad Ali. Could I fight off the champ? The facts were simple: If he wanted to see something in me, he would see something in me.

I considered simply calling him and telling him I couldn't make it, but I was concerned about how that would sound to him—a lot like I didn't want to make a sitcom, if it was my talent he was interested in. At 6 P.M., after much debate, I threw on an unflattering outfit and got in a cab toward midtown. If Will Smith was gay, I was going to find out the hard way.

Planet Hollywood was packed. Jam-packed with white people. I took a cursory look around and saw no black people, which gave me pause. As I walked up to the hostess, I realized just how ridiculous the question I was about to ask was.

"Is Will Smith here?"

"Yeah, I think he is in the back corner."

Suddenly, I relaxed. Here I was, thinking he was gay and wanted to fuck the shit out of me, and in reality he was suffering fans while he waited for me at a table for two. I felt overwhelming embarrassment as I walked to the back of the restaurant, but when I got there I saw no one.

I walked back up to the front and told the girl I couldn't find him.

"You mean like the mannequin?" she replied, assuming that I was the most die-hard Will Smith fan—someone who would only eat there if he could have a table close enough to his replica.

"No, the person."

"I'm sorry?"

"Is Will Smith *the person* here?"

"Is the actual movie star, *Will Smith*, here at Planet Hollywood? Having dinner? *No*, he is not."

"Do you have a reservation for Will Smith, for two . . . in a movie theater?" I tried.

"In a movie theater? Sir, we are an establishment dedicated to Hollywood, with mannequins of movie stars and memorabilia. The actual movie stars themselves do not hang out here, and we do not have a movie theater."

I realized just how crazy I sounded when she spelled it out, but I wasn't done.

"Do you mind if I sit here for a little while and wait for him?"

"Seriously?"

"Seriously."

"Knock yourself out."

As I sat in the waiting room of the restaurant, I could hear the hostess and her colleagues mocking me. She asked a passing waiter if he had any tables with Will Smith at them, to which he responded, "Yeah. He's sitting with Kevin Kline and Marvin Gaye." That carried on for the next ten minutes until, from behind me came a six-foot-six, 350-pound black man. His eyes panned the waiting room until they met mine. "You Bert?"

I nodded yes and he motioned for me to follow him downstairs. All I could think as I followed him was, "I pray to God I don't have to fuck this guy, too. I bet there is a lot of dick in those pants."

He led me to the bottom of the stairs and showed me to a small room. "In here," he said. I stepped into the small room to find nothing but the red velvet curtain that encased it, a folding table, and nine black men waiting for me.

My heart dropped. *I thought this was just going to be me and Will,* I thought. The idea of fucking one man I could wrap my head around, but fucking ten? I stood in the doorway with my mouth wide open. I offered a smile but was met with none in return. As I walked in, they stopped talking and started staring at me. The 350-pounder (I later learned his name was Charlie Mack) left without an introduction—not that I minded. I was too busy doing the math: nine black men, Will makes ten, and I'm sure he is bringing Jazzy Jeff, which makes eleven black men that I will have to fuck, all on a folding table.

We waited silently for what seemed like an eternity as I pondered how many yards of black cock would be passing through me that night. I stood motionless with my back to the wall not making eye contact, the way white people do when they are being stared at by black people.

Until, to my surprise, the Fresh Prince himself walked in with, you guessed it, Jazzy Jeff and three other friends that were, thank God, of smaller stature. By this time I was mentally lining them up in order of size and line placement for what would be the longest game of leaky submarine ever played.

Again, Will lit up the room—everyone smiled. He put his arm around me, announcing, "Everyone, this is Bert, the guy I've been talking about so much."

My heart sunk as they smiled and began to move in on me. In panicked moments like this your brain thinks faster than normal. My brain whispered, "Get on your knees." I figured I would definitely rather go for a clean-up-free, no-harm-no-foul blow job than a that-was-awkard-but-fun-sorry-you-are-crying butt fuck. I was about to ask Will if he wouldn't mind going first and saving Charlie Mack for last, when I felt the curtains behind me brush my heels. They opened and everyone in the room moved past me. I turned to find the most impressive personal movie theater I had ever seen. Will, arm still around me, said, "Grab two seats, I'll get us drinks."

I grabbed the best two seats in the theater—middle row, center—and before I could say "Parents just don't understand," he showed up with two Long Island Iced Teas. He leaned over and whispered, "Crazy room for a hip-hop fan."

"Huh?" I muttered.

"Biz Markie, Kool Moe Dee, Jeff, Charlie Mack."

They were all there. They had been there since the beginning. I was too preoccupied with sizing up the lump in their pants to look at their faces. Will, in our dance studio meeting, had listened to me explain what a huge hip-hop fan I was and decided to pull some strings and get all the greats in one room for me to meet. I had been seeing more feet of cock to bear when in actuality I was living a hip-hop fan's wet dream. As the movie started, I thought to myself, *I could have fucked Kool Moe Dee?*"

The movie was *American Pie* and I laughed liberally, hoping that Will would think I was connected with what the youth of America found funny. When Jason Biggs put his dick in the pie, the room full of brothers groaned. Will leaned over to me and whispered, "You believe that?"

I whispered back, "I did that to a McDonald's cheeseburger once."

I regretted saying it until Will laughed. "And that is why we are doing this deal!"

At the end of the movie, we sat around finishing up cocktails and getting ready to leave when Will put me on the spot. "So Bert, what was your favorite part of the movie?"

I wanted to say, "The part where I didn't fuck fifteen black guys." I opted for, "The Stifler character. Every white guy knows a guy like that, and it was played brilliantly." Biz Markie mumbled something about white people that I couldn't decipher, but the others heard it and fell apart.

When we walked up the stairs, all I could think of was how badly I wanted that same hostess to be at the top. As luck would have it, we crested the stairs and there she was. When her eyes met mine, I nudged Will and said, "The hostess is a huge fan of yours." Will smiled at me, slid over to her as only a mega movie star could, flashed his million-dollar smile, and said, "One love! One love." Her mouth was agape. Before following him out, I whispered, "The movie theater is downstairs."

A few weeks later, the deal was closed and we sold a show to FOX. We wrote it, and a year later they passed on it, as they do with most development deals. But I learned a lot from Will in that year. He taught me two of the most important lessons in Hollywood: how to take a general meeting and how to sell a TV show. He also validated my existence in Hollywood. Because of Will's belief in me, CBS signed me the very next year to another development deal, and the cycle started all over again. This time I ended up shooting a pilot alongside Elliott Gould. Elliott and I got along really well. So well, in fact, that at the end of production I walked into my dressing room to find a note with a phone number on it that said, CALL ME, ELLIOTT. I called him and he said, "You are an interesting young man, very talented, we should get to know each other. Do you like seafood?"

I heard my dad's voice. "I think he wants to fuck you, buddy."

8.

A Honeymoon You Can't Refuse

My wife was pregnant when we got married. We hadn't planned on it, but upon hearing the news we were both elated. We were in our thirties and well past the time where something like that was truly an accident. I knew LeeAnn was who I wanted to spend the rest of my life with, and now she had to. We found out she was pregnant the day after we moved in together—the same day, coincidentally, that I had convinced her to take a Xanax and down a pitcher of margaritas with me while we painted the living room.

We told the doctor on our first prenatal visit and she smiled at us. "As long as that's not a lifestyle type of thing your baby is going to be fine."

For who? was my first thought. That was *exactly* my lifestyle at the time. But my wife, who rarely drinks and hasn't taken a Xanax since, heard that as a mandate, and thankfully so. What I heard was that I had a designated driver. We told our friends that night, she told the girls, and I told the boys who responded by handing me a glass of absinthe.

I took no part in planning our wedding, not because I didn't care, but because I am suspicious of any man that does. Weddings are a woman's dream, honeymoons are a man's. She wanted to get married in her hometown so we were getting married in her hometown, which was so small and so Southern that question four of our marriage license application was, "Are you blood relatives?"

The only time I did step in on planning was when my wife asked me whether we wanted to dance or to drink at the wedding.

"Are you fucking kidding me?"

"We can't have both because in my hometown they believe that the two together lead to sin."

"What is this, *Footloose*?"

"We gotta pick one."

My answer came quickly. "I pick booze, 'cause I'm dying to see them stop me from dancing."

Like I said, my focus was the honeymoon and considering I was already partying for three, I paid great attention to the planning. I didn't want to fly—I knew a flight would cause more anxiety than necessary, on one of the most anxious days of my life. Our wedding was in her hometown of Bowdon, Georgia, which meant our options were even more limited.

There was also the fact that I was close to broke. Lee-Ann didn't quite know it yet—that was information I'd share after our commitment ceremony—but all the TV money I had been gifted as a youth was running close to dry. I scoured the Internet looking for honeymoon options and came up with nothing. But my concerns were lifted at the eleventh hour when my dad called.

"Buddy, I got the place for your honeymoon."

He had been talking about my honeymoon situation with a friend, and this friend said he had just been to the most amazing, quaint resort. It had blown his mind. We could get a discounted rate, he added. My dad told me he had already taken the liberty of booking us a place at the resort, so as not to lose out on the opportunity. We were locked in. I asked him what the price per night was, and he said it was around thirteen hundred a night regularly, but with the deal he was getting for us, it was going to be a steal.

Once we heard the details, we were sold. There were only thirteen rooms on the island, and every room was a treetop bungalow with its own outdoor shower. Everything, he told me, was included—booze, food, activities.

All you had to do was show up and you would be taken care of every step of the way. It sounded too good to be true.

I told LeeAnn, who was shocked at the thought of paying $1,300 a night. She had already paid for our entire wedding, which cost $5,000. So a honeymoon that out-spent that amount was no small thing. But I assured her with my dad's hookup, which was almost half off (I was guessing), and not having to buy plane tickets, it was a totally affordable plan. She conceded, I called my dad, and it was done.

Our wedding was beautiful, a true testament to red-neck ingenuity. It was like CMT and TLC had teamed up. We were married at the church across from her grand-parents' house the day after Christmas. It was catered by everyone who loved her. LeeAnn's grandfather smoked several hams for pulled pork. Her granny and aunts put in at least eighty hours in the kitchen, making potato salad, Brunswick stew, and cole slaw. We had two wedding cakes, one made by her cousin and another made of Krispy Kreme donuts and Moon Pies. My dad ate himself sick and my mom danced like it was *her* wedding (LeeAnn's dad got special permission from her small Baptist town for us to both drink and dance).

The next morning we said good-bye to our families, hopped in my mom's car and drove south toward the

Florida Keys, hauling ass and excited, like we were picking up a kilo of coke. Our destination was a place called Little Palm Island.

Many hours later we pulled up to the valet at Little Palm. As a joke, I asked the valet if he had ever met a famous person before, thinking he might be curious or even stunned by my question. He was not.

"Yes, they come here all the time," he said as he reached for the keys to my mom's car.

"But who is like the biggest, though? Because, you know, I'm on TV. I don't want this stay to be awkward."

"Evander Holyfield was here last week."

"The prizefighter?"

"Yeah, the prizefighter. And you just missed Debra Messing."

My wife laughed as he took my keys. "We'll keep your car on the mainland," he said. He left us at check-in holding our bags with me holding my dick in my hand.

We both suddenly felt out of place. If what the valet had told us was true, then this place was obviously a five-star place, and here we were in shorts, flip-flops, T-shirts, and sunglasses we had gotten at a gas station earlier that day. Our bags didn't match. To top things off I was holding a case of Budweiser under one arm like Uncle Eddie from *Vacation*.

But as we approached the front desk from the valet, I still beamed with excitement. There's nothing I love more than starting a vacation and this was a big one, the kind prizefighters and movie stars took, and I was getting it for half off.

I lowered my sunglasses and like a true sophisticate announced to the man behind the counter that this was our honeymoon. He forced a smile, congratulated us, and offered us the island's signature cocktail, called a Gumby Slumber. I'm not sure exactly what was in it—rum, juice, bean shavings, coconut, perhaps. I grabbed both, gesturing toward LeeAnn. "She's pregnant but I'll take hers."

Within moments we were checked in. But I was confused. Where we had pulled in was just off the main highway that takes you from Miami to Key West, and all around I saw nothing that resembled a five-star hotel. No treetop bungalows in sight. That is when the clerk motioned us to a dock.

"The boat out there will take you to the hotel."

"The hotel isn't here?"

"The hotel is on a private island, sir."

"A private island."

"It's very nice. You won't be let down, sir."

We left our four mismatched suitcases at the front desk and walked out to the dock, where we found a boat straight out of the 1920s waiting for us. I secured the Budweiser under my arm, grabbed LeeAnn's backpack, and we hopped on.

Just as we were about to take off we heard someone

from the check-in area call out to hold the boat. The captain obliged, and we waited until on the dock appeared two of the most uptight, upscale, white-bread New York socialite-yuppie types I had ever seen. They had matching pastel sweaters tied around their necks, brand-new Birkenstocks and Revo sunglasses, and both held armfuls of designer bags from what looked to be an extensive, recent shopping spree.

They literally did a double take when they saw LeeAnn and me. They actually turned their noses. This was a couple we would never hang out with. They were the complete and total opposite of everything we stood for.

The two sat directly across from us. Short introductions were made before they took great pleasure in telling us everything we needed to know—that he was an investment banker, she was an art dealer, that they *badly* needed this vacation because things were absolutely *hectic* for them. It was *so hard*, they said, to really take time for themselves these days. They had, in fact, been shopping in Key West and spent way more than they expected, but why do you make the money if not to spend it? It's a *vacation*, right? After listening to their résumés for half the boat ride, the woman asked us about ourselves. I took the bull by the horns.

"I'm a comedian and she manages the apartment building we live in. Which is great because we don't have to pay rent. We just got married. Oh, and she's pregnant."

That was the end of that. They looked at us as if we were a couple of Somali pirates who had just hopped on the boat, then went through the spoils of their shopping spree, always keeping a careful eye on us. I cracked open a Budweiser and we all enjoyed the silence.

When the boat pulled up to Little Palm Island, I nearly tripped over LeeAnn's jaw. A new concierge had come to greet us at the dock and give us a tour of the island. It was amazing, possibly the nicest place I have ever been. Manicured lawns, treetop bungalows, a gorgeous pool, a private beach, a top-notch fitness center and spa, a library, and a restaurant. Everything was private and everything was over-the-top. The tour couldn't have taken more than twenty minutes—the whole island was only five acres—but with every turn you took, something new impressed you. I kept waiting to see a prince or a president.

The concierge directed us to our bungalow, which overlooked the ocean and was set twenty feet up in the trees.

When we got to the door LeeAnn grabbed me and whispered, "They've carved our name in the door."

She was right. These rooms didn't have numbers, they carved your names into the fucking door. He let us in and it was absolutely gorgeous. Dark teak wood floors, white, plump couches, and a huge California king bed set upon a frame made out of reclaimed lumber from a shipyard, with a mosquito net draped over it. Big, slow ceiling fans spun in every room, but I didn't listen to a word the concierge said after I passed the outdoor shower. There is something absolutely magical about bathing yourself outside, and to me the idea of hot water in the cold morning air was something you only read about in books. I was naked before he even left the room, singing in the treetops as I cleaned every inch of my body. I cracked another Budweiser and walked in from the shower to find Lee-Ann inspecting the room.

"This is going to be expensive."

"Don't worry," I told her. "My dad got it hooked up. We're paying next to nothing for this. Zilch. Zero."

"The guy that showed us around said that khakis and collared shirts are mandatory for the men at dinner along with close-toed shoes. Did you bring those?"

"Yes, of course."

"He said the menu is set by the chef and you eat what everyone else eats. He also said if we'd like he can set a table up in the ocean."

"What?"

"That's what he said, but you have to pay for it."

"I'll pass," I said.

It was getting close to dinner time so I threw on my khakis, a collared shirt, a pair of shoes, and walked with LeeAnn over to the restaurant. As we made our way to our table and I sized up the other guests, I could tell beyond a doubt that we didn't belong. We were not only younger than the average guest, but I assumed from the fact that some of them were in suits and evening wear that we were in a considerably lower income bracket. I remember being obsessed with the fact that it looked like they had all just showered. It seemed odd to me, this must have been some kind of rich-person behavior, considering I don't usually shower when I'm on vacation. As I saw it, the beach was a shower, as was the pool. Maybe they were as obsessed with their outdoor showers as I was. Anyway, I may not have been like them, but I sure as hell could smell like them. My only saving grace as a broke comic walking around a room of upper crusters was that my new wife was banging hot. I dumped all my insecurities into that fact.

We saw the two dorks that had taken the boat to the island with us and matched their fake hellos with fake hellos of our own. He was dressed in a suit with a bow tie and she was in a dress just shy of an evening gown. I played a little mental game that I often play called What Do They Look Like When They Masturbate. It's a fun game to play, especially in a room like that. And for him I envisioned it perfectly. His masturbation was something he succumbed to and didn't delight in. It was fast and necessary, filled with guilt. His secretary had a slip of the nip and he couldn't control it, and when he was done there was a harrumph, as if he'd let himself down. She on the other hand didn't masturbate at all, as she was averse to pleasure, thus explaining her marriage to him.

We were seated outside and as soon as we arrived at our table, a Key deer walked up to greet us, as if it had been cued by the hotel staff. But it wasn't. LeeAnn lost her fucking mind and started feeding it, which apparently was something everyone had already been briefed on. They stared as if LeeAnn had started shoving the cutlery up her asshole. An older woman quickly reprimanded us, saying that we were not to feed the deer under any circumstances. What other circumstance would there be, I thought to myself, other than one just walking up to us.

"How can anyone not think that a small deer coming up to your table and wanting a snack isn't an absolutely amazing life experience?" LeeAnn said to me.

I ordered a bottle of wine—with one glass—and we did what most couples do on dates: We eavesdropped on everyone else's conversations. Our food arrived and shortly after, we heard the woman who had reprimanded us ask to speak to the chef. The waiter obliged, and LeeAnn leaned in. "This can't be good."

"You think she saw him feed a deer?"

When he came out, she said five words while pointing at her plate.

"You are better than this."

I'm sure the chef had a bunch of words himself that he'd like to share with that lady, but he apologized and promised a better meal the next day. LeeAnn and I were appalled but were too busy wolfing down our meals to be bothered with whatever small detail in the recipe that had pissed her off. So when the waiter asked what we thought of dinner, we told him that the woman was out of her fucking mind, and the meal was possibly the best meal we'd ever had. And it was. Everything there was mind-blowing. The wine, the views, the service, the privacy.

But the people that were vacationing on this island could suck hot homeless dick for all I cared. I'm not sure if it was because we were outsiders, getting all of this opulence at a discounted rate, so we were easily satisfied. But it seemed that everyone we'd run into was more disgruntled than the last. I'd never paid four figures a day for a room (I still haven't), so maybe being an asshole just comes with the territory. I'd probably be pretty pissed off, too, if I knew that every moment of a vacation was putting me deeper in the hole. Anyway, that wasn't the case for us.

After dinner we retreated back to our cottage, I took another outdoor shower, and LeeAnn filled out our breakfast menu for the next morning.

That next day the most amazing thing happened. We woke up comfortably around eight o'clock and I heard a noise on the front deck. I opened the door and saw what I thought was the same Key deer scamper off the deck and down the steps. In front of me was a table set for two with breakfast waiting for us. I swear to God, it was like the deer brought it to us, walking on his hind legs, holding it on his head and front hoofs. I told LeeAnn breakfast was outside and she couldn't believe it. We walked over in our robes, sat down, and to my astonishment, it was piping hot. To this day I have absolutely no idea how they did it, but every single morning, the second we'd open the door, breakfast was waiting for us at a temperature that suggested it had come directly from the kitchen. And every single morning there were Key deer watching us like the Little Rascals, waiting for us to slip up and leave our meals unattended just long enough for them to snag a bagel. We finished our breakfast, got dressed for the beach, and headed in that direction.

We were the first ones there that morning, but to our confusion every single chaise lounge had someone's bag on it. Every chaise lounge except for one. Not a single soul was on that beach, yet every single seat had been spoken for? These fucking disgusting rich people, we found out later, would wake up at five in the morning, claim their spots on the beach, then go back to bed and come back when they were comfortably rested. It absolutely blew my mind what these rich fucks were capable of. Is this the behavior you have to assume in order to amass millions? When they started showing up around ten o'clock, I saw that the woman who had claimed the most chairs was the same woman who had chastised the chef the night before. I wanted so badly to walk over to her and say, "You're better than this." But the truth was she might not have been.

I gave LeeAnn the last seat, and I stood in the water with a Gumby Slumber, staring back at my wealthy neighbors.

And that was how just about every single day went down. We would get down to the beach earlier and earlier, still to find only one seat available. As people showed up I would try to guess which bag matched their outfit for the day and guess which seats they had "called" before sunrise. I would be left standing in the ocean, facing everyone with cocktail in hand, telling LeeAnn stories, while everyone eavesdropped. As the week passed, it seemed more like I was doing stand-up for the group than talking to just my wife. Until one day everything changed.

Halfway through our stay, a thunderstorm of a man and his lightning rod of a girlfriend showed up on the beach. They looked to be straight out of the *Sopranos*. He was a large man with tattoos in places so odd I thought they must have been earned rather than bought, while she had the unmistakable figure of a onetime stripper. The first morning they came to the beach, LeeAnn and I were already there, but the others hadn't arrived yet. He looked around and saw that every seat had bags on them, and with a shrug of his shoulders and a "What the fuck" muttered under his breath, he threw the bags off of the chairs he wanted. Come ten o'clock when the woman who had chastised the chef (every single night now) found her stuff lying in the sand, she asked the group, passive-aggressively, "What happened to my bags?"

The man looked her straight in the eyes. "They were on my fucking seat."

"Oh no, you're mistaken, sir. We called those seats."

"Doesn't look like it's working out so good for you."

"But we woke up early and put our bags on those seats so we could have them."

"Take that shit back to Connecticut, honey. What you think this is, high school? When I'm done with my book you can have your seat."

And that was that. There was no more calling seats after this man arrived.

My stand-up got a little louder each day, as I stood in the ocean facing LeeAnn and hoping to God this guy would recognize just how funny I was and take me under his wing. I wanted this guy to like me more than anything in the world.

Until this point, LeeAnn and I felt like the black sheep, but now that these two were here, we were in the clear. He would sit on the beach in black shorts, a black Tommy Bahama shirt, black sunglasses, and a black hat while his chick downed champagne in a skimpy bikini, tearing through Marlboro 100s. And in some sort of Darwinian turn, the disgusting rich-people tribe started to warm up to LeeAnn and me. It was hilarious, watching them try to connect with two people they had turned their noses up at.

One of the women handed LeeAnn a James Patterson

book, *The Big Bad Wolf,* while I was at the bar. "I got this for Bert."

"You got Bert a book?"

"Yeah. I thought he might enjoy reading a book on the beach like the rest of us."

"Unless it's got rum in it, I don't think he's going to touch it while he's here."

When I got back to the beach with another drink, Lee-Ann was forced to tell me about the present the woman had gotten me, in front of her. She couldn't keep the laughter out of her voice. "Bert, this lady was nice enough to get you a book."

"What for?"

"I think she wants you to read it."

We held in our laughter. We were like two kids who had just smoked weed before study hall. I thanked the woman profusely and poured on for over an hour about how much I loved dogs. You can imagine my embarrassment when later I found out that the Big Bad Wolf was a serial killer and not a canine.

As the week carried on, I got no closer to meeting the two people we had now found were named Danny and Dawn. We'd see them at the beach, and I'd passed by them on the way to the bar, trying to get Danny interested in me with some witty one-liner or a comment about how nice the island was, but like I was a fat chick on spring break, not once did he even notice my existence. Our second to last day, we took a boat ride with a new young couple. It was a sunset cruise, the martini of boat rides, and they were actually fairly decent people. They were our age and, from what I could gather, he came from money. He and I drank on the boat like pirates trying to get rid of the clap, as the captain sailed us around the island. We watched the sunset, and on our way back in, began talking about the mystery couple. They, too, had noticed Danny and Dawn and had been just as fascinated as LeeAnn and I were.

"He's got to be in the Mafia, right?"

"Definitely," I said.

"Do you think those tattoos mean anything?"

"They have to. They are in too odd places not to."

"You talk to everyone; what is he like?"

To their dismay, and my own, I explained that I had not been able to break the ice with this man the entire trip and I had absolutely no idea what he was like, beyond standoffish, overweight, and banging a hot stripper. We spent the rest of the ride back to the island fantasizing about what their lives must be like back home.

We got back to our cottage and I took yet another shower. I was finding so much enjoyment in that shower that the treetop animals must have thought I had OCD. We went to dinner, we came back, I took another shower, and we went to bed.

The next morning was our last full day on the island

and much to my chagrin, Danny and Dawn were nowhere to be seen. I spent the day like I had spent the previous five, standing in the ocean, drinking the signature drink of the island, and working on new material to the crowd of eavesdroppers. That night, LeeAnn decided she was going to allow herself a glass of champagne, so we found a couple of Adirondack chairs on what we thought was a secluded part of the island, facing the sunset, and we ordered an expensive bottle. Just as we opened it, Danny and Dawn came walking up behind us on their way to the dock to take the boat ride we'd taken the day before. As they passed behind us, I shouted to them, "Boat ride?"

Great opener, Bert. State the obvious, pose it as a question, and open your eyes real wide.

They said nothing and kept walking. My first attempt failed, but I knew for a fact that when they were done with their boat ride, they would have to walk past us one more time. We sat and drank champagne and I planned my attack. We saw the sunset, I killed most of the bottle and switched to beer, and by the time they walked back past us, I was well lubricated, locked and loaded with a better intro line. When they were the perfect distance away, I perked up out of my Adirondack chair like a gazelle who had just heard a lion fart, and I motioned to them.

"Hey guys, come on over and have a drink with us."

They said nothing. Assuming that they didn't hear me, I tried again.

"Danny, Dawn, come on over and have a seat and a cocktail with us."

I saw the look on Danny's face and realized that there was no reason why I should know their names.

"Do I know you?" he called out from twenty feet away.

I was busted. I looked like a stalker now—or worse, an undercover cop. Picture me on my feet, holding a beer, in board shorts and a tank top, a look of dumb shock on my face.

"No, I'm Bert and this is my wife, LeeAnn. We were just wondering if you guys wanted to sit down and have a drink with us."

Danny stayed back, dressed in the same black-on-black beachwear he had been wearing all week. "We're good," he said curtly.

And they left. I felt like a complete and total asshole, but at least I had given it my best shot. As we headed back to our bungalow, LeeAnn and I imagined what the night might have been like had we hung out with them. We got back to the cottage, LeeAnn began to get dressed for dinner, and I went to do the thing I loved doing most on that island, namely, taking an outdoor shower. My genitals by this time had been washed red, my hair turning brittle, my feet forever pruned. I was shocked when LeeAnn came out and stopped me before I could get in.

"Danny and Dawn invited us to their room for drinks before dinner."

"What?"

"Dawn was just standing outside our bungalow, shouting for us. I went out there and she said to come down immediately, they were ordering cocktails for us."

I quickly threw on the clothes I had been wearing and we made our way to their bungalow. When we got there, we were stunned. It was three times the size of ours, two stories, hanging over the water, with a dock surrounding it. *Mob money must be slamming,* I thought to myself. Their bungalow was also easily three times more expensive-looking than ours. When we got to their door we noticed their names weren't on it.

"Typical Danny. He likes his privacy," I said, as if I had known him my whole life.

"I know, right?"

We knocked on the door and Dawn greeted us in jean shorts and a bikini top.

"I'm fucking so glad you guys could fucking make it. Sorry about Danny earlier, he don't fucking like nobody."

From the background we heard Danny yell, "No, I just don't like the fucking people on this island." Danny then appeared from one of the many rooms in their bungalow in a wifebeater and his black shorts. "They're all stuck-up cunts if you ask me."

Wow, I thought, we are getting to see Danny be Danny. It was like going to a wedding with Sammy Davis Junior and watching him dance drunk.

He stuck out his hand. "I'm Danny, this is my chick, Dawn."

"I'm Bert, this is my chick, LeeAnn."

"I'm his wife," LeeAnn corrected.

"My first wife."

Danny let out a roar of a laugh, put his arm around my shoulder, and walked us into his living room.

"I told the bar to send over whatever the fuck it is you've been drinking all week."

I looked over and saw a spread of booze that looked like it belonged in the Puff Daddy suite. Two bottles of Cristal on ice, a bottle of Johnnie Walker Black, beer on ice, wine opened and breathing, and pitchers of Gumby Slumber.

We sat down and Dawn poured us all drinks.

"No, thanks," LeeAnn said.

"You don't drink?" she asked.

"No, I do, but I'm pregnant."

"Oh, how long have you guys been a married?"

"Five days," I said.

Danny started smiling. "You guys ain't like these fucking people at all, are you?"

"No, we are not."

LeeAnn looked at me. She could hear my accent shifting into Danny's as I matched him in tone, energy, and personality. I tend to do that from time to time, mostly around black people.

"How you fucking affording this?" he said.

"My dad got us a deal."

"Ain't no deals on this island, kid. Everything's over-priced and everything has a price tag on it. What do you do?"

"I'm a comedian, she manages an apartment building."

"Real fucking people, I love this. A comic and a slum-lord."

Dawn popped a bottle of Cristal and poured me a glass, and despite the fact that I was already holding both a Gumby Slumber and a beer I had brought from our room, I gladly accepted it, as I figured this might be the only time I would ever be able to drink Cristal.

She looked to LeeAnn imploringly. "Are you sure? It *is* Cristal."

"If there's one thing I know about LeeAnn, it's that she loves champagne," I said.

"It ain't gonna make a fucking difference to the baby; my second wife drank a glass of wine every night when she was pregnant," Danny said.

Sage enough advice for LeeAnn, I guess. "I'll have a small glass," she replied. We all smiled.

We got to know each other. Danny was in the con-crete business. He told us he'd been "pinched" in a town very close to where LeeAnn grew up, which confused my literal wife. "Who pinched you?" "A cop," Danny said flatly. "Why would a cop pinch you?" Danny almost laughed the tattoos off his plump frame. Danny never said anything about the Mob or being in the Mafia, which only fueled my speculation that he was. As I kept drinking, I saw every detail of his life through my Mob glasses.

Dawn, despite having the body of a stripper, had children almost our age. She steered the conversation all over the place, hopping from subject to subject at high speeds. She mostly talked about her psychic abilities and the fact that she knew our child was going to be a boy and a Gemini (it was neither). I talked at great length about myself, and Danny seemed sincerely interested. He loved comedy and loved the fact that I knew the material, off the top of my head, of all the comics he loved. I was so excited to be hanging out with them that I wasn't paying attention to what I was drinking, or how fast I was drinking it. While LeeAnn kept the same small glass of Cristal in her hand, I was juggling beers, champagne, rum, and now Johnnie Walker Black like a bear in the Russian circus. We talked so seamlessly and effortlessly that we didn't realize how much time had passed until Dawn looked at her watch.

"Oh shit, we're gonna miss dinner."

"Fuck it, let's go. You guys want to eat with us tonight?" Danny said.

"Sure," I said. "We'll go down and get changed."

"Fuck that shit, were going like this." Danny stood up. If Danny wasn't concerned with the dress code, then neither was I. I looked to LeeAnn, who shrugged her shoulders.

"Fuck it," she said.

There are three moments in my life, now as a forty-year-old, that I wish had been videotaped. My first home run. The first time I did stand-up. And the moment, that evening, when I walked into a five-star restaurant with Danny, Dawn, and LeeAnn, wearing board shorts, flip-flops, and a tank top. Slow motion, a mismatched foursome who looked like they were straight out of Daytona Beach central booking. Oddly enough, I was the nicest dressed of the bunch. LeeAnn was in little more than a cover-up, from having been at the beach all day, Dawn was still in a bikini top and jean shorts, and Danny was wearing black shorts, a wifebeater, and house slippers. Before the maître d' could say anything to us, Danny slipped a hundred-dollar bill in his hand.

"Table for four," he said.

The best part was the look on the faces of the couples we had been interacting with all week as we walked through the restaurant. They were dressed in suits and ties and dresses, and here we came like a group of shipwrecked sailors who had stumbled onto their island paradise. As we passed the couple we had been boating with the day before, their eyes lit up with excitement. We had cracked the code. I could tell instantly they wished they were with us. The couple we had talked to on our way to the island was appalled, by the look on the wife's face. It was as if we had spit on their food. But best of all was the woman who had reprimanded the chef. On the way to our table, Danny lazily stopped at theirs to find out what was on the menu for the evening.

"Oh shit, Bert. It's fucking steak," he yelled across the restaurant.

I matched his energy. "We're eating like fucking kings tonight, Danny!"

I was already drunk when we sat down at the table, but the first thing Danny did was order shots. Of all the times I've been drunk, this night would rank in the top five drunkest. (Just so you have the rest, in no order: pledge night for ATO; camping in eleventh grade; the night I discovered Southern Comfort; my oldest daughter's fourth birthday.) LeeAnn was noticing. She kept pulling on my shorts and telling me to slow down. But I was with Danny. I was a made man, and the people on this island knew it. Anyone that served our table got a hundred-dollar hand-shake. The waiter came over more that night than any previous night. The chef came out and Danny greeted him with a hug, then slipped him a hundred-dollar bill and told him he wanted two of everything.

The night was just getting better and better. When LeeAnn went to the bathroom, they would go on and on about what a great woman I'd landed, and when I'd go to the bathroom, Danny would come with me and on the way we'd get a drink and a shot at the bar, and he would explain the importance of tipping. He would point out the people he didn't like and he'd tell me why. And from what I could see from his insights he could have worked at a fair doing this.

"See a guy like that right there? He holds his fork like he is nine. Guy's got no fucking culture. Guarantee you his parents were drunks.

"See that tall guy in the tan suit, with the fat wife. A guy like that—with this kind of money, in his kind of shape, his kind of height—doesn't think the rules apply to him. He fucks around on his wife. Look, you can tell by the way he's not listening."

He credited his insights to years on the street, and having to be able to read people in a second. He was shocked at how good I was at it, although my skill didn't hold a candle to his.

One of the four or five times we stopped at the bar, the husband from the sunset cruise approached Danny and me to buy us a drink. But before he could even say hello, Danny was gone.

"How are you guys hanging out with them?" he asked me.

"They invited us down for a drink."

"And the restaurant let you guys in dressed like that?"

"Yeah, I can't believe it either."

"What's he like?"

"Cool as shit!"

Before we could finish, Danny was barking my name from across the restaurant.

"Yo, Bert! Our fucking steaks are here!"

And just as promised, I found two steaks waiting for me.

Danny decided to take our drink game to the next level. It started with a three-hundred-dollar cognac that to my shock even LeeAnn wanted to try. I downed mine and Danny ordered me another. This is when everything gets real fuzzy. Apparently I started to tell everyone that someone was trying to kill us—me, specifically—which Danny found hilarious and I found even funnier. When I get really drunk I get really giggly and Danny took great pleasure watching me giggle myself into fits of laughter. I took fifty-dollar sips of cognac. Danny laughed harder than I've ever seen a human being laugh. Which obviously made me laugh. His face was red, his belly jiggled, and he kept yelling at the top of his lungs, "I fucking love this guy! I fucking love this guy!"

In a way, this is what I'm about, the urge to get someone who I don't have much in common with to laugh. It's one of my favorite things to do and it was the highlight of that night. I was sitting among a bunch of self-important millionaires, and I was not only hanging out with the most interesting man on the island but cracking him up beyond belief. I don't know exactly how long our night lasted, but I can say that LeeAnn cut it off just in time to get me outside of the restaurant so I could throw up—which I did the entire walk to our cottage. She took me upstairs and put me in my beloved outdoor shower where I puked up two steaks and a bar's worth of liquor. I howled under the running water with more laughter and vomit like a drunken Tarzan until my body gave out and I was put in bed.

Our phone rang continuously that night. Danny wasn't done with me. He and Dawn had fallen in love with us and wanted to spend more time together once I was done throwing up. LeeAnn politely declined on our behalf.

The next morning I woke up feeling like I was coming directly out of intestine surgery. I walked out onto our porch to find not only our breakfast and a Key deer, but our bill for the weekend. As I opened it, I was a bit nervous, but also curious to know how much money my dad had saved us. I stepped inside to hand it to LeeAnn, then headed back out for my last outdoor shower.

She came out with the same look she had on her face the day she told me she was pregnant.

"We could've bought a car instead of coming here?"

"What?"

"It's $15,000."

"That's got to be wrong," I said. "We got a deal."

I heard Danny's voice in the back of my head. *Ain't no deals on this island, kid.*

"Did they charge us for last night's drinks?"

"No, Danny paid for all the drinks."

"Then there must be a mistake."

LeeAnn got on the phone and called the front desk back on the mainland and found that there had *not* been a mistake. In fact, there had never been a deal. My dad simply booked the reservation for us and assumed they'd give us a deal because we were on our honeymoon.

I called my dad and explained the situation. From where I stood, I would be paying for this honeymoon for the rest of my life. Most couples get married and take a while to accrue this kind of debt, but LeeAnn and I managed it in five days. My dad told me not to worry, that he would call the hotel and take care of everything, and to enjoy our last morning. It was tough to enjoy the place knowing now how much it cost. I went out to my beloved outdoor shower, but it just wasn't the same, I could see the water bill rising with every extra second I took. The beach seemed even worse when you considered the free ones out on the mainland. They were just as nice and you didn't have to jockey for seats. I went to the bar and asked for the first time how much my Gumby Slumbers were.

Fifteen dollars. I got a bottle of water (five dollars). And to think I had been using those to wash the sand off my feet like the other patrons.

So we packed up our belongings and left. I contemplated packing up one of the Key deer and selling it on the mainland—surely you could get a couple grand for it—but I couldn't find one. (They always knew when it was time to hide.) LeeAnn called Dawn one more time to thank her and Danny for the spectacular dinner the night before, and to apologize for my behavior, but Dawn seem to think my behavior was the best part of the night.

"Are you kidding me? We love you kids! You gave us the most fun we've had the whole time we've been here."

We took the boat back to the mainland and I gave the concierge my credit card, telling him to charge as much as he could on it, explaining that my dad would be calling him shortly to deal with the rest. But he told me it had already been taken care of.

My heart dropped. *Had Danny paid our bill? Was I now indebted to him?* I saw it all unfold in front of my eyes. He'd call me one day and ask me to drive a truck full of cigarettes from L.A. to New York, and I wouldn't be able to say no. He'd be subtle, like, "You just dropping them off like the boat guy from Little Palm Island . . . you remember Little Palm Island, don't you, Bert?" Next thing you know, we'd be chopping up a body in the basement of his buddy's mom's house in Jersey, and I'd be asked all the time to recite Sam Kinison bits to all his friends.

But as I got in the car to drive back to Tampa to catch our flight home to L.A., my cell phone rang. It was my dad. He apologized for booking me into a hotel that cost more than I'd made the year before and said that he had put it on his credit card and would take care of it. LeeAnn and I thanked him profusely and I asked if he needed me to do any "favors" for him. He declined. Just drive safely, he said.

To this day, if you ask LeeAnn or me about our wedding, there are three things we bring up. First, the incestual inquiry on our marriage certificate. Second, how expensive our honeymoon was. And last but certainly not least, our dinner with Danny and Dawn. I'm not sure what Danny is up to these days—if he's still in concrete, or if he is in fact *in* concrete. If he's still with Dawn, if they got married, or if they both moved on. I hope he's seen one of my TV shows and I've made him laugh a little, the way I made him laugh at dinner that night.

More than anything, though, I hope he doesn't remember me. And that when he saw me on TV, he would say to Dawn, "That kid is funny; I bet we'd get along with him and his wife." Because if he remembers my name and LeeAnn's, and if he's reading this and is in any way insulted, I'm afraid I may wake up one morning to find a Key deer in my bed.

9.

Shermfest

The night I met Tracy Morgan, I got hit by a bicycle. It wasn't a chain-around-the-chest, hot-roddin' bike messenger, but a flowery-basket-on-the-front, ring-ring type of bike driven by an attractive brunette. I was working at the Boston Comedy Club, standing out front "barking," trying to bring people in to watch our comedy show, when I took a step into the street. I had checked the traffic headed one way, in the direction of West Third and saw nothing. Then *wham*.

She had slowed down enough not to kill me, but not enough to *not* knock the living shit out of me. I got up, and as you'd expect in New York, she began yelling at me.

Still a bit dazed as I got up off the ground, I said nothing, and eventually she left.

I spent the next ten minutes overwhelmed by two observations. One, that *she* was pissed off at *me*. I was the little fish in this scenario, getting muscled by the big fish, and the big fish just told me to go fuck myself like an abusive husband, and I was the battered wife who took it. Two, that our paths had started twenty odd years ago in completely different places—different states, maybe different countries—and we had spent our last two decades weaving our ways to this point on West Third Street. Always a romantic, I couldn't get past the serendipity of it. How we traveled, struck one another, and continued our traveling.

None of this would have occurred to me if she had been fat. Funny how meaningful an event can be when the person you have it with is attractive. Had she been a fat chick, I probably would have been in the hospital but seen no hidden meaning. Regardless, I spent the remainder of the time before that night's show focusing on how I could turn this bit of kismet into a kismet bit.

My focus shifted when I saw Tracy Morgan walk up to the club. At the time, Tracy was just beginning his reign at *Saturday Night Live* and he had the strut of a fourth grader coming back from the principal's office. The comics at the club said he looked healthy, which seemed odd to me because he didn't, but apparently this was an improvement. They also told me he was hilarious, which I believed because just watching him interact was comical. His mouth would purse, he'd laugh loud, then stop suddenly and stare at the person, lift up his shirt and rub his belly, then embrace the person and walk away. He walked right past me into the club. Within minutes, he was back on the sidewalk, holding court with some black comics, one of them my friend, Tony Woods. Tony was older than me, and a much more seasoned comic. He was the guy I spent every night with—drinking, deconstructing life, talking comedy. I felt honored that Tony had taken an interest in me. It was well known that ten years earlier he had taken another comic under his wing, and that comic was Dave Chappelle. Tony definitely rubbed off on Dave stylistically. They were *very* similar on stage. The difference was that Tony remained the same person offstage. Dave did not. And as Dave shot to stardom, Tony remained behind, in the trenches.

Always the friend, Tony motioned me over and introduced me to Tracy Morgan.

"Yo Tray, this is my man, Bert, but I call him Sugar Bear."

Tracy gave me a long stare, a mean mug, and a nod, and continued the conversation he had been having. Making sure not to overstep my bounds, I went back to barking, only this time with much more ammo. "Hey guys, we have a great show tonight. Tony Woods, D.C. Benny,

Judah Friedlander, and from *Saturday Night Live,* Tracy Morgan."

By the time Tracy hit the stage I had brought in enough patrons to earn myself a few minutes to watch a pro at work. At this time in my career, anyone who had made it out of the clubs and onto TV, but who still came back to the clubs to work out material, earned all the respect I had. So I stood in the back and watched as Tracy Morgan took the stage.

"Alright, we all do crazy shit," he opened a bit. "Same shit, crazy shit. Yeah. Yeah. Alright. Alright. Who remembers finger-fucking by the handball courts?"

The crowd stared at him, simultaneously turning their heads in the way of the confused. Their drinks sat still on their tables as if they were confused, too. If "finger-fucking by the handball courts" had been a defining moment in Tracy's childhood, one thing was clear: it had not been for this audience. Sensing their reluctance to identify, Tracy tried again. "You know you remember that shit, don't you?" A couple of really white people, who were uncomfortable with the fact that a TV star wasn't getting a laugh, chuckled, giving him permission to dig deeper. His focus now was directly on them.

"You do remember that shit, don't you?"

Silence from most of the people, except the white table who still giggled uncomfortably, like you might while the host of a dinner party slaughters a chicken for you.

"You post that bitch up, back against the wall, and just pussy pop that bitch."

Tracy has an undeniable talent for losing himself in a character. He acted out the scene, throwing one arm against the brick wall of the club, "pussy popping" an imaginary woman.

"*Bam, bam, bam*, just pussy poppin' that bitch!"

Jaws dropped. He lowered his head and talked directly into the mic now, soft and intimate.

"Arm against the wall, head in yo jacket, smelling yo own stank."

By this point, I was lost in the imagery, imagining a pre-*Precious* Precious staring at the passersby as Tracy aggressively finger-fucked. Despite the fact that I had never taken part in said activity, he was getting me there. I felt like I was one of his classmate friends, holding a basketball, waiting for him to finish so we could wrap up our game.

On my way back to work outside, I heard, "Yeah, I need a fat bitch, with stretch marks and a C-section scar."

The way I heard it at the time, Tracy had booked *SNL* having never performed in front of white people. He was forty pounds heavier, and wore a red, blue, and yellow beanie with a propeller on it. Did he do this material? Did he do impressions? Or was Lorne Michaels so insightful that he could recognize genius even when a crowd couldn't?

After ten minutes, Tracy came out of the club bubbling.

Maybe he was expecting his friends, but finding me, he opened up. "Damn, that was hot. Yeah, real hot."

Not sure how to respond, I simply agreed. He smiled, looked up and down West Third Street, and said five words that would transform that night.

"Yo, you wanna get high?"

I have never said no to that question, even when I wanted to. I am exactly the person they were referring to when they talked about peer pressure in seventh grade. Now as an adult, I find it outright rude to tell someone who has taken a chance and told *you* that they do drugs and would like you to partake with them, "no thank you," that you are better than them and will not partake in said activity. Another thing to know about me, as well as yourself, and about life in general: If you've never gotten high with a black man, you are not living the way God intended.

The list of black comics I've gotten high with looks like the set list for a Def Jam reunion show, so before Tracy could finish his sentence, I'd already said yes.

We walked west and took a left on the first side street, Sullivan. As we walked, Tracy did none of the things the other black comics did, like fill the air with small talk—about their set, or about the chick they planned on fucking that night. He walked silently, like a soldier, to a place I would know we had reached only when he'd decided we had.

It occurred to me that I had no idea what "getting high" meant to Tracy Morgan, so you can imagine my relief when he reached into his pocket and pulled out a joint. It looked like the work of an amateur—crooked like a croissant, like a joint that had been rolled at Woodstock and had been dodging fire ever since.

Tracy looked around, lit it, and hit it hard. He then passed it to me. I nodded and took an equally hard hit.

I should note that everything that follows is hazy and suspect. I've heard this story told back to me many times, and it's never the same, nor am I ever as innocent as the last time I'd heard it.

As I inhaled, I sensed instantly that something was amiss. This didn't smell like weed and it definitely didn't taste like weed. I looked at Tracy with confusion. "What is this shit?"

He smiled. "What is this shit?"

"Yeah, it tastes weird."

"Oh, you never smoked sherm before?"

"Sherm?" I said.

"It's wet," he said as he hit it again.

"Wet? What are sherm and wet?"

He rolled his eyes and started walking back to the club. "So you never smoked PCP before?" He laughed, disappearing into the foot traffic of West Third.

The answer was *no*. Not only had I never smoked PCP, I had also never been offered PCP. There were a lot of things I wished I could have told him. Like, for instance, "Hey, when you smoke PCP with a person you just met, you might want to ask them if they would, in fact, like to partake of your PCP, rather than just assuming that they are hip to the fact that the joint you possess is indeed 'wet.'" Also: What fucking year is this that we need to add PCP to our joint to improve our buzz? Had this been 1978 and we were two kids at a Molly Hatchet concert trying to share a handjob from an old lady who had just been dumped by her Hell's Angel boyfriend, I might have gotten it. But it was 1999, and weed was fucking awesome as is.

I walked back to the club hyperaware of what I was feeling, which was mostly panic. From what I knew about PCP, any second now I was going to be covered in spiders.

I entered and went directly to Tony Woods. I pulled him aside and urgently whispered, *"I just got wet."*

"Then dry the fuck off."

"No, sherm-wet. I smoked wet sherm."

"What the fuck are you talking about?"

"I smoked PCP with Tracy Morgan."

"When?"

"Five minutes ago."

"No, you didn't," he said.

"No, I did. Tracy asked if I wanted to get high, and apparently when he says 'get high,' he means PCP and I said yes not knowing it was PCP, and we smoked a joint that tasted funny and it was sherm, he said."

"Tracy doesn't smoke PCP."

"No, he does and he did, and I did, too."

"No, he doesn't, I promise you. He's just fucking with you."

"But he said it was PCP."

"No. He's fucking with you because you're white."

"Really?"

"Yeah, you're white and you probably made some weird white-guy comment, like you do, and Tracy thought he'd play you, and now you're played."

"Really?"

"Yeah, look at you. You were about to call an ambulance, and all, 'Tony, I'm wet, I'm wet!' Take a deep breath and relax."

I took a deep breath. "So I didn't smoke PCP?"

Tony took a second and thought about it. "Probably not."

"Probably?"

"I wouldn't go home if I were you."

This panicked me. "Why not?"

"Because I know you, and if you go home you're gonna sit in your apartment and start to think you're on PCP. So stay with me and I'll watch you."

"What are we going to do?"

"We're just gonna drink and keep cool."

I went on stage that night. Or maybe I didn't. If I did, I bombed. And if I didn't, I did and I bombed.

What I know for sure is that Tony and I ended up at a club called Madame X. Madame X was, and maybe still is, one of the many clubs on Houston Street. One of those clubs where you have to walk down a small flight of stairs to enter, and the second you do, you feel like you're in a different world. Red velvet walls breathed in and out, as you pulsed like blood toward the back of the club.

And in the back that night, there was a one-man show going on called "Tracy Morgan: Real Talk." Tracy was holding court for any and every black man that would listen. There were twenty by the time I got there.

"Here is the thing you need to know about Tracy," Tony said to me. "He doesn't give a fuck. TV, film, none of that is why he's here. He's here because he's real, and all these niggas know that. He's famous, but he treats all of them like they ain't no different than him, he just got money."

And by the display of champagne bottles that littered the surrounding tables, that was clear. Every time the waitress walked by, Tracy ordered more like someone was going to prison the next day. "One more bottle. Fuck it, make it two!" The tab, I assumed, was so sizable, it could easily swallow a couple of Heinekens, but regardless I snuck over to the bar and paid cash for my drinks. I wasn't used to this kind of hip-hop decadence, but I had definitely heard about it. Tonight I had a front-row seat.

Tracy is the kind of unbridled genius that comics automatically appreciate. On stage, reins are forced into its mouth, but at a club, around friends and half in the bag, his genius was in full gallop.

"I got a pretty *dick*. You can suck it with the lights on, *and* I don't even have to know your last name!" The phrase stuck with me. I had never thought about how much of my sexual activity took place in the dark or at night, or with strangers. How ashamed we are of our bodies, and how vulnerable we become when we get naked in front of strangers. I tried to recall any oral sex I had received in the light from a girl whose last name I didn't know. To present my body in full display, either with overhead lights or in sunlight, and to allow a woman to get so close as to perform a direct examination, made me chuckle in embarrassment. I felt like telling him he should write that down and work it out, because there was definitely something there that people could relate to, but I got the feeling he wasn't about to slow down and pull out a pen and a notebook. He was on a roll.

Everything he said that night was a diamond, but a blood diamond, because as the night continued, a small fortune of alcohol accrued on that table. At the end of the night, when the only energy left in the club was Tracy's, the white waitress appeared through the crowd of brothers with a smile and a bill. She quickly scanned the crowd—landing her sights on me, the lone white guy. Tony chuckled as she handed me the bill and my asshole tightened. Was I going to have to itemize this bill and ask everyone what they ordered and tell them how much to chip in? By the time it was in my hand, it was clear that she assumed I was going to pay, because, by her assumption, I was the one white dude with a mess of black men, and therefore I had to be their lawyer, or agent, or coach. As I fumbled to explain I wasn't the man she was looking for, Tracy's eyes wandered my direction. Here, he popped off.

"Ah, fuck that. I'm the rich nigga in here!"

Nervous for a second that I would get stuck with the bill, I smiled.

"Fuck that white boy, he works the door!"

Dissed, but fine with it, I nodded at the waitress. "I'm not on this bill. I was buying drinks at the bar." Too preoccupied to listen, she was pulled back into conversation with Tracy.

"Hey bitch, I'm talking to you!"

This got her attention. She quickly handed the bill in his direction.

"No, fuck that shit. How you going to disrespect me in front on my mans and dem? I'm the rich nigga in here! I'm on TV!"

Whatever Tracy's goal was, it was working. Now the whole bar was watching—including the bouncers, two ex-NFL linemen, who were standing close by.

"I apologize. Here you go, sir," she said.

At "sir," the group of black dudes hissed like it was a slam-dunk contest and she had just missed.

"Oh, now I'm 'sir'? Couple of minutes ago I was just some nigga who couldn't pay a bill, but now I'm 'sir'?"

"I wasn't being racist," she said.

"But you gave him the bill 'cause he's white. He ain't got no money! Why didn't you give it to me? 'Cause I'm a nigga. But I'm a rich nigga! I'm on TV!"

At that, Tracy ripped off his shirt and threw it in her face. And just like that, the bouncers were on top of him, standing so close they cast shadows over him. Tracy was no more than a quarter of their combined weight, but that didn't scare him. As they stood there, the bigger of the two spoke his last two words of the night. "My man."

Tracy looked at him with disgust, smiled discreetly to our group, and answered as if he was seven feet tall. "I ain't yo man," he said, and threw a punch.

This is when I snapped back to my reality: I was *definitely* on PCP.

I quickly stood up, looked at Tony, who was trying to break up the fight, and walked directly out of the bar. I passed people who were just now realizing that a fight was going down, but I knew there was a tsunami coming and I was headed for high ground.

I quickly made my way up the stairs two at a time and as I stood on Houston, pacing, I kept thinking to myself, *This isn't happening. None of this.*

After two minutes of waiting, I turned west to head home, when Tony exited the club. "Damn, Sugar Bear, shit going off!"

"Really? Is he winning or losing?"

"What do you think?"

"Should we wait?"

"I say we give him a minute."

We stood there for what couldn't have been more than forty-five seconds, when the doors of the club were burst open—by Tracy's head. The bouncers held him limp, shirtless, parallel to the ground, and threw him up the short flight of steps. He landed on the sidewalk, his body lying at Tony's and my feet as the doors shut behind them.

"Shit, shortie," Tony said. "What are we gonna do with a dead Tracy Morgan?"

A second later, the doors flew back open, and a shirt came flying out, just like in a cartoon, landing directly on Tracy's back.

In moments like this—in intense situations *or* when you're possibly on PCP—time slows down so much that you can see a hummingbird fart. I looked over to my mentor, who was dumbfounded. In all the time I had known Tony, I had never seen him nervous or fazed. But looking at him that night, with a near-dead *SNL* star at our feet, I could tell we were up shit creek. Was this how the world would know me, as the last person to get high with the famed *SNL* star? I'm sure they would do a toxi-cology report, find the PCP, and blame it on me, the hanger-on, the starfucker who was a bad influence on this vulnerable man. There laid my comedy career dead at my feet. I'd be like the stripper partying with Farley or that chick who killed Belushi.

Then, just like that, Tracy was on his feet. He took his shirt, snapped it clean, looked at us, and smiled.

"Now *that* is how you get out of paying a check."

Crazy as a fucking fox, he walked east toward Broadway. "That's how I know you didn't smoke PCP," Tony said. Tony joined Tracy, looking back at me. "You coming?"

I shook my head no, and smiled. "I'm heading back to my apartment."

"You okay?" Tony asked before they disappeared.

"I'm fine," I told him. I headed west toward home.

I walked home and passed the Comedy Cellar, praying to see someone hanging out outside who I could share this amazing story with, but no one was there. I made the rest of the walk home feeling oddly sober—not high at all, not even drunk, but happy.

In fourteen years of doing comedy, my path has crossed with countless comics, many of them repeatedly. But never again have I met Tracy Morgan. I'm sure he wouldn't re-member me at all. Guys like Tracy formed my constitution as a stand-up comedian, not the other way around, so really, why should he remember? Sometimes that's how it's meant to happen. Your paths begin in very different places, cross for one crazy moment, and then continue on.

10.

CP

I was twenty-seven years old and boarding a flight from LAX to JFK, returning home to New York. I was buzzed from drinking at the airport bar, and as all single young men do, I was hoping for a seat next to a drop-dead gorgeous model. Looking down at my ticket as I moved past first class, I quietly seethed as it occurred to me that all the models were probably behind me. I had an aisle seat, on the two-seat side of a 767, and my odds were as good now as a power hitter's piss test.

Ahead I saw what could only be described as a hotter, more unique-looking Sarah Michelle Gellar. I quickly tried to do the math, simultaneously praying that the open seat next to hers was mine. As I got closer, I saw that—somehow, miraculously, like a hole in one—it was.

I slowly approached the row and put on my most casual voice as I murmured the obvious, "21B, 22B . . . This must be me!" I put my stuff in the overhead as I strategized my pimp game, but as I sat down next to her she jumped into conversation before I had the chance to start.

"I have my cat at my feet. I hope you don't mind, or I can trade seats with someone else." Truth be told, I am deathly allergic to cats, and had she been twenty pounds heavier, I would have gladly swapped her out. But she was so hot—the kind of hot where you don't realize whether she has big tits until the second date. I told her how much I loved cats, how I couldn't live without them, how I had no problem with her cat meowing two feet from me, shedding its poisonous fur onto me, for five hours. She beamed at how much we had in common. She rescued cats and this was her latest project. Her name is inconsequential (mostly because I'm now a married man, and I can't remember any woman's name but my wife's; speaking of which: If you are reading this, honey, now would be a great time to stop), but what was important was that she grew up on the Upper East Side of Manhattan, was obsessed with Guns N' Roses, and within five minutes of meeting me, asked if I wanted to split a Xanax. I obliged, because I'm a gentleman and because the refusal of a casual drug offer is rude. We carried on the most seamless, carefree, hilarious conversation I've ever had on an airplane. Turns out, that's what Xanax and wine will do, and we drank wine freely. I talked a lot about myself, which anyone who knows me can attest is fairly common. The trade-off was that halfway through the flight, she asked if she could take her cat out from under the seat and let it sit on her lap. I gently grinded my teeth as I forced out a yes. The idea of what I knew to be a poisonous animal sitting inches from me, staring its shock-filled eyes into mine, ran panic through my heart, but not enough to overwhelm the Xanax or the effects of her hotness, so I obliged, and it did sit on her lap—for about two minutes. Then it found a nice place to nestle in between us. Thankfully the bag of cocktails circulating through my system kept the inherent, obsessive itchiness of my allergies at bay, but as we landed I could feel myself giving in to the dander.

We taxied to the gate and said good-byes at our seats as my eyes began to swell. I darted up and grabbed my bag, but before I exited the plane and headed to the bathroom to give myself a sink scrub, I did something very out of the ordinary for me. I asked for her number. I've never been a guy who could make himself vulnerable like that. I grew up at a time when placing a phone call to a girl meant something, and that feeling will always stay with me. Asking for a girl's number always seemed to come with a sly wink, as if you were saying, "I'd like to have sex with you. I understand there are some hoops I gotta jump through and this is one of them, but I'm willing and I'd like to start now." It must have been the mix of highballs and drugs, but I took it a step further and told her I would like to get together tomorrow night for some more highballs and drugs.

She smiled and gave me her number, and I skipped to the bathroom to wash myself.

At baggage claim I saw her name on a placard held by a chauffeur and thought, "Wow, the mystery. I should have let her talk a little bit and learned more about her, as opposed to razzle-dazzling her with the B-Man pitch. Who is she? What does she do, other than rescue cats, eat pills, and drink? Or is that enough?"

I claimed my bags, got in a taxi, and, as I have done with every woman I have ever longed for, I dreamt of the life we would have together. One time I met, offended, then scared off River Phoenix's sister while I was working at a Barnes and Noble in New York. I hadn't recognized her when she walked up to the information desk, so I asked her where she was from. She told me Gainesville, and being from Florida, I lit up. She said her last name was Phoenix and I naturally asked if she knew that River Phoenix was also from Gainesville. She said, "Ahhh, no." I said, in all seriousness, "The famous dead guy—you didn't know he was from Gainesville? And you guys have the same last name!" She walked away, understandably upset. Some people might have seen the exchange as a sort of BRIDGE OUT sign. I saw it as an in. For days I talked about the possibilities we had as a couple. Because I was *real*.

The same tornado was starting all over again, only this time it was way more tangible. The girl from the airplane was all I talked about for the next twenty hours. She had explained on the plane that she had a friend in town and they had already made plans to have drinks in SoHo, but she would love for me to meet up with them. I convinced my two best friends, Huicho and Tony, to accompany me. I suspect they agreed only so they could have proof of how much I exaggerate every aspect of every detail of every story I ever tell. But as we walked into a crowded Mexican bar in SoHo, I saw Tony's Cuban mouth drop.

"Holy shit, you weren't kidding. She's ten times hotter than Sarah Michelle Gellar."

My buddy Huicho kept whispering to me as we got closer to the table. "Is she the hot one or the hotter one?"

"The hotter one," I said confidently as we navigated our way through the crowded bar to the table she and her friends had held for us.

"I'd fuck her in front of my wife," said Tony (who, coincidentally, is now divorced from said wife).

We sat down and proceeded to have a picturesque night of cocktails, laughs, and debauchery, as we stumbled our way from one place to the next along the uneven cobblestones of SoHo. We clung to each other in a big

St. Elmo's Fire–esque group, laughing, carousing, and ca-
vorting. At the end of the night, she gave me a quick kiss
and an odd little smirk, and slid into a cab with her two
friends. As Tony, Huicho, and I walked back to the West
Village, Tony revealed in a drunken stammer a detail he
had coaxed from her friend.

"Fuckface. Your girl is a trust-fund kid. Old New York
money that isn't going anywhere."

Huicho said, "I knew something was up when I went
to shake her hand and she extended her left one out like
royalty."

I smiled to myself. I had hit the lottery: a hot trust-
fund kid with hot friends, and she thought I was about as
fascinating as I thought I was.

The next night we did the exact same thing. More
friends, loud bars, and even more drinks. We ended up at
my local watering hole, The Room, a dimly lit, two-room
establishment that played great music and served strong
beers. Huicho's girlfriend, Alex, met up with us after a
ridiculously long day on Wall Street, and she gave me the
same approving grin as I introduced her to the group. She
pulled me aside as the rest of them found a place to sit and
asked, "Alright, what's wrong with her?"

I laughed and felt a moment of pride as Alex and I
walked to the bar to order drinks for the group. The night
ended just the same as the previous—quick kiss, odd
smirk, and into a cab. I walked home with Huicho and

Alex, who spent the entire walk asking questions, doing what all girls do: trying to pick apart a pretty girl.

"Why did she extend her left hand when I met her?"

"She's rich," shouted Huicho into the empty sky. "Blue blood, that's what they do."

"I don't know," Alex said. "Something seems odd about her to me."

Huicho and I laughed off her questions as female cattiness and suspicion. As we walked home through the streets of the Village, I told them everything I felt for this chick I had known for three days. We all got home—I was living with the two of them at the time—and made our favorite late-night snack: a dozen poached eggs.

The next morning I was awoken by a very grim-looking Huicho, who said we needed to talk. "I think you need to go out on a sober date with your girl, during the day, in the light."

"Why?"

He stood beside my bed. "Something is wrong . . . I'm not sure what it is but there is definitely something wrong with her."

"Be more specific."

"I just think you should go out on a date—sober— with her. In the sunlight. Get a good look at her."

"Just tell me what you're trying to say." I was exhausted from his accusations.

"Nothing. I'm just saying you're falling for this girl

pretty hard, and you've only been around her black-out drunk."

"Are you trying to say she's a dude?"

"No, not at all. Definitely not a dude. I just walked home with you last night and the things you were saying about her were pretty big statements coming from you. I've known you since we were kids and I think, if you feel the way you say you're feeling, you should have a sober date with her and see if you guys have anything in common other than the fact that you both like getting black-out drunk and stumbling around lower Manhattan."

"Who the fuck goes out on sober dates?"

"You two should. Take her out Sunday, pick her up at her place, see where she lives, just you and her, and get to know her."

"I know her, Huicho. I sat next to her on a plane for five hours."

"Drunk and on Xanax. And if I know you, she didn't talk at all."

He knew me well. "Fine, I'll call her now and see if she wants to go to brunch on Sunday."

Which I did. I called her, and she was not only more than happy to hear from me but we talked on the phone for an hour like eighth graders. I worked that night and met up with her and some friends uptown at an Irish pub, and we literally didn't move from our corner booth until closing time when we were too drunk to stand. We split ways, promising to see each other the next morning, but those plans seemed ridiculous to me. I had done my best detective work at the Irish bar: no Adam's apple, big tits, a great smile. Her friends were real. She did admit that she had run away with one of the friends we were having drinks with, an equally hot girl, when they were young. But I had done the same in first grade. (Of course they'd hidden out in Brooklyn with some street kids, since she lived in New York City, and I had just stayed in my front yard tree for about an hour.) She partied a little with drugs in college—but who hadn't?—and had made some bad decisions when it came to men, which I thought was playing to my favor, as I was asking her to continue that streak. Everything seemed on the up and up, and that is exactly how I explained it to Huicho as I left for my church-ass sober brunch date the next morning.

"Good, I'm glad you're happy," he said.

I walked out the door and headed uptown. I had a hard time figuring out what to wear to a brunch and opted for a pair of light khakis, flip-flops, and a plain T-shirt. It was summer in New York and Satan's-taint hot. I remember because when she answered the door at her family's house, the first thing I noticed was that she was wearing running shoes with a sundress. Running shoes, I thought. What an interesting choice. How far is this restaurant? Did she just get done running around town? Should I have worn running shoes? Maybe it was a Northeastern thing, like

Londoners and their trainers. She asked me in to introduce me to her family, and that's when I noticed it. A
pronounced limp. Like a big dog who has gone on a long
hike, or a grandmother getting up to make another cup of
tea during a commercial break. The introductions to her
dad, grandmother, and brother were a blur as I thought to
myself, "Why is she limping?"

We left and walked around the block to her favorite
restaurant, and the limp remained constant. We sat down
at our table and I noticed her smirking at me, the same
smirk I had gotten at the end of each night. But now it
came all the time. The waiter gave us water—a smirk. I
said the place was nice—a smirk. I asked her where the
bathroom was—a smirk. My head started spinning: The
limp, the smirk. Then it hit me like a ton of bricks. She was
eating only with her left hand. Cutting with her left hand,
forking the food with her left hand, lifting her glass with
her left hand. Everything with her left, the right hidden
under the table. Curiosity was overwhelming good inten-
tion. I stopped the waiter and ordered a Bloody Mary, and
that's when she said it.

"Cerebral palsy."

Apparently she had been born with cerebral palsy,
though she was fairly high functioning, and she completely
assumed I knew. How could I not?

She kept telling me about her life, but all I could think
to myself was, what does this mean for me? Did this

change anything? Did this make her less attractive to me, and if it did, what did that say about me? Was I a bad person for not noticing until now, and would I be a bad person if I let it affect my feelings for her? I drank four more Bloody Marys, finished the meal, smiled politely, and limped her home. I then hopped in a cab and headed back to my apartment.

As luck would have it, everyone was awaiting my arrival like it was Christmas morning. Tony, his wife, Huicho, Alex, and Huicho's sister Val, all stopped talking as I walked in the door. I realized instantly they had been talking about me. I stood in the doorway of our living room and announced my findings.

"She has cerebral palsy!"

The women processed the information, nodding, while the guys laughed hysterically.

"How big of an alcoholic are you that you go on four dates with a chick and don't even know she has cerebral palsy?" howled Tony.

"I think it shows how little he pays attention to anyone but himself," Huicho said.

"So it's over," proclaimed Tony.

"Nope. I invited her to go to Scotland with me," I said, shocking even the women in the room. They all knew that the next week I had to fly to Scotland to perform at the Edinburgh Fringe Festival with three other New York comics.

"I told her I was leaving in a week, and I'd be in Scotland for a month and it sounded a lot like 'I just realized you have cerebral palsy so this is over,' and I felt like a jerk, so I told her if she wanted she could come with me."

The room sat in shock. "Is she?"

"Yup. She said she has always wanted to see Scotland. She goes back to L.A. tomorrow, and I'll see her in two weeks in Scotland."

I left the living room and walked into my room. I felt good. I was an okay-guy after all. Yes, I had a drinking problem. No, I didn't pay attention to anyone but myself. But when push came to shove, I wasn't about to let a non-progressive disorder of the nervous system tell me who I did and didn't like.

The next time we spoke was over the phone and this time I asked her to tell me more about herself.

"I'm a vegan, and you should know I have severe urges to firebomb Pink's."

"Pink's, as in the hot-dog joint?" I said.

"Yeah, Pink's, as in the purveyor of death, hatred, and all things meat. Have you been there?"

The answer to that question was yes. In light of the fact that she was considering a terrorist act against them, I decided to hold off on telling her that it was maybe the best hot dog I had ever had.

"I can't even believe that anyone can enjoy meat," she said. "Do you know what I mean?"

"Well, people have different likes and tastes."

"Have you ever had veal?"

"I fucking love veal!"

I realized what had just come out of my mouth. The fact was, I liked veal so much that when I heard the mention of it, my Paleo instinct took over and I didn't have time to edit.

"Are you serious?"

"Uhhh . . ."

"Do you know what they do to those babies?"

The truth was I didn't even really know anything about veal. All I knew was that I'd had veal parmesan a couple times, it was on the short list of things I wanted to regularly put in my mouth, and just the mention of it made my mouth water. For the next thirty minutes she lectured me on the atrocities of veal raising, how they tether them in crates to restrict their movement, to make them more suitable for assholes like me, who joyously shove hate down their throats. At the end of the lecture she gave a mild apology. Then she started crying. Talk about the joys of sobriety! Things had been going much better when we talked about me, we drank, and when she didn't have cerebral palsy. She apologized. I didn't need the apology, but I took it. I told her I'd see her in Scotland.

I hung up the phone and told Huicho I needed to talk to him, so I offered to buy him dinner. Over a nice Italian meal I told him my conundrum.

"How do I get out of this? I'm sure she was spewing this crazy before but I never listened. The only thing I've heard her say in this past week is, 'hot dogs are death, veal is murder, and I have cerebral palsy,' which is night and day from 'do you want to share drugs, you are fascinating, and I have a cat.'"

As with most male relationships, he did nothing more than say, basically, "I'm glad I don't have to make that decision." We drank together until it wasn't bothering me.

The next day as I was packing for my trip, my cell phone rang.

"I may not be able to make it to Scotland," she said.

I exhaled and began envisioning a great joyful swim to freedom. "The problem is that I rescue cats, and I have someone who is willing to watch all of them but one, my problem cat."

"How many cats do you have?" I said meekly. I realized I had never told her I was deathly allergic.

"Right now, five."

"Five cats. How awesome, and they all live in your house?"

"My apartment in L.A., yes. So, I'm just giving you the heads-up, I won't know about Scotland until tomorrow."

"Umm, okay, but that creates a little bit of a problem, because I'll already be in Scotland. Do you want me to try and call you, or do you want to try and call me?"

"I'm not promising anything. Let's play it by ear."

That was good enough for me. I wrote it off as a problem averted, and that night I got on a Virgin Atlantic flight to Edinburgh and drank like a king. To this day I'll never forget that takeoff into the night above Manhattan, soft and smooth on the top deck of a 747.

The next morning I sat in a flat, still drunk from my flight, sharing my exploits with Patrice O'Neal, one of the comics I was staying with. Patrice was older, larger, and blacker than me. He howled in laughter as I told him the story.

"You gotta talk about this shit on stage! You start dating a cripple and don't even know about it 'cause you're such a goddamn drunk? And then she is fucking crazy and you can't dump her 'cause now you know she's a cripple!"

I laughed it off. I knew Patrice well enough not to let on that it was bothering me. Patrice was an old-school bully who loved to watch people get uncomfortable. That coupled with the fact he was a genuine comic genius meant that if he wanted to, he could dismantle you like a puzzle, so not even you knew where your corners went. He liked me enough to let it slide, and that was the last I heard about it—until the next day when she knocked on our door.

My heart sank when I saw her at the door, tired, drunk, and with more bags than expected. I slowly walked her into our kitchen, where she met Patrice for the first time. The beautiful thing about Patrice was he didn't accept bullshit. If you came to him with something ingenuine, he sensed it. He also relished playing the part you expected of a man like him—a six-foot, 400-pound black man with chipped front teeth, who scowled more than he smiled. I introduced the two of them and as Patrice extended his right hand and she reached out with her left, I could almost hear Bruce Buffer's voice in my head: *Let's get ready to rumble.*

"What am I supposed to do what that shit, kneel and kiss it? What are you, a fucking queen?"

Patrice walked past her in a huff and went directly to the freezer. I immediately regretted having told him anything about her as I heard him pull out a pack of hot dogs.

"Bert, you want a hot dog?"

"No thanks, I'm good."

"How about your girl? I can make chili dogs with some bacon bits, cheese. Mmmm. Sounds good, don't it, Bert?"

I could see her eyes growing red with anger, and I grabbed her by the good arm and escorted her to the living room. There I introduced her to Rich Vos and Patrice's girlfriend, who was from England and staying with us. I then walked her into my room, where I hid her from Patrice until showtime.

Around eight o'clock, we all hopped in a cab together and headed up to the Assembly Hall, where we were performing. Patrice said nothing, as his chick and mine were apparently hitting it off, both, coincidentally, wearing extremely sexy leather pants.

We sat in the back of the hall and watched as Rich Vos slurred his way through his set, followed by Lewis Schaffer. Just before it was my turn to take the stage, Patrice leaned over to me and whispered in my ear, "Your girl looks hot in them pants." I exhaled a deep breath, thinking the worst of the storm had passed. "Too bad you know there's a baby leg in there."

I took the stage and bombed. So did Patrice, which unbeknownst to me was about to make the remainder of the night absolutely unbearable.

We went downstairs to a bar all the comics from the festival frequented, and I noticed our two ladies were well past tipsy. Not fifteen seconds into sitting down, my chick made the mistake of mentioning how she had expected Patrice to be better on stage.

She didn't hear it, but I definitely did: It sounded like the click of the land mine you just stepped on.

She continued talking about his set and where she thought he lost the audience. I could see a smile growing on Patrice's face. It was as if someone had cut off a serial killer in traffic, and he was now following her home. She stopped for a second to take a sip of wine and Patrice began what I can only call the most perfect disassembling and reconstructing of a person's insecurities and flaws, in the most casual and offhand manner, that I have ever seen. He was loaded with information I never thought he would use, because had I ever thought this would happen I would never have told him anything about her. But as it was, I had told him more than he needed, and he used it all. Phrases like "Upper East Side pussy" and "liberal ass limp" decorated his work. The evening ended with her screaming about him in my bedroom, which I'm almost sure he could hear.

The next night was worse, and the night after that no better. He had her number and he was going to continually pull it at his leisure. This made her crazy—and absolutely unbearable to be around. At one point I thought he was going to make her racist. She would get drunk and fight all night with Patrice, so much so that after a week I started to think she really wanted to fuck him. Then when Patrice didn't feel like fighting anymore, she would come into my room and fight with me. It all culminated with her standing naked at the foot of my bed, shouting at the top of her lungs, "You are never gonna fuck me!" (Which I didn't, as a matter of fact. We never even kissed the whole time we were in Scotland.)

Then God intervened. One morning, two weeks in, I got a phone call from my manager telling me three things: I got another TV development deal, I got a TV show on

FX, and that I had to fly to L.A. immediately. The news couldn't have come at a better time. Not only were great things happening for me in Hollywood, but I had a reason to leave this horrific reality show.

Patrice came out that morning as I was trying to arrange flights. He had a smile on his face as he told me that he had stuck his head into my room last night, as she stood naked in front of my bed (I had seen him). I smiled back and told him, "Well, she's all yours."

"What?"

"I just got a deal and a TV show. I have to fly back to L.A. tonight."

Patrice spent the next hour and a half taking me apart over breakfast, which he made, slowly. He explained why my show wouldn't succeed, why my deal wouldn't make it, and why he felt bad for me as a comic. I half brushed it off and half took it to heart.

I'm not proud of what I did next but I stand by it: I left. I left her with Patrice and I left Patrice with her. They called a couple times—once while I was at a bar in Santa Monica and another time while I was looking at houses—both times still from Scotland, to bitch about one another. Patrice ended up kicking her out of the flat and she ended up backpacking through Europe. I started my TV show and didn't hear from her once. But I felt bad about how everything had gone down. That's what I do, I run away from problems.

Until one day I decided to make amends and reach out. I'd learned that I was going to be interviewing Slash of Guns N' Roses, and to make up for being a complete and total dick, I told her she could come by the set. She jumped at the offer, and we talked on the phone for twenty minutes like nothing had ever happened. The next day she arrived, and I had a production assistant find her a front-row seat for the interview. Slash arrived shortly after. The supervising producer pulled me aside and asked, "You have booze in you greenroom, right?"

"Yeah, of course."

"Can we get Slash a drink?"

"Fuck yeah," I said. Next thing you know, I'm pouring two glasses of brandy, one for Slash and one for me, as he's telling me about how his chick had made him sleep on the couch the night before.

She was seated up front, on the floor with the crew, and she watched me do possibly the best interview of my life. I was a fan of Guns N' Roses, too, and I asked Slash all the questions they had told me not to. That, coupled by the fact that we were drinking brandy out of coffee mugs, only tightened our bond.

Directly after the interview he looked at me, still on set, both of us still mic'd. "Hey, I have to fly to Europe in a few hours and I can't go home. Any chance I can get another one of these?" he said, pointing to the brandy.

The crew stiffened as I took him back to my green-room. I subtly motioned for her to follow us and as I did, I saw her body lighten with joy.

We entered my greenroom, and I poured all of us cocktails. We sat and drank for half an hour, and for the first time I finally let this girl talk. She asked Slash all the questions she had always wanted to. They beamed back and forth at each other as Slash, historically silent, suddenly rambled.

I took pride as I sat back and truly listened for the first time in a long time, sipping my brandy. After one round of drinks she looked me in the eyes, expressing what I assumed was gratitude, and gave me that all-too-familiar smirk. She then asked me very politely where the restroom was. I told her, trying desperately to express the same gratitude back through my eyes, hoping I had repaid my debt—of not knowing she had cerebral palsy, acting awkward when I found out she did, lying about hot dogs, eating them even more often behind her back because it was fun, leaving her with Patrice, never calling again. She stood to exit, and as she did I realized just how prominent her limp was. How did I ever *not* notice it? Anyway, did it really matter? She was just a chick who wanted to be loved, like any other. As she left the room she grabbed the door with her good hand, reaching across her body, and shuffled awkwardly out the door.

As she left, Slash grabbed my arm. She exited, the door closed, and he looked me in the eyes and said, "She is absolutely perfect."

I was shocked. He was *not* seeing exactly what I had *not* seen on the plane, and those first few nights of drinking. He was probably as drunk now as I was then. He set his coffee mug down in front of me, and whispered through his hair, "I'll take one more."

As I filled both our cups I could hear Patrice's taunting, maniacal cackle in the back of my head. I imagined him howling with laughter. "Both you muthafuckahs didn't see that shit? Damn, Bert! You as big of a drunk as Slash!"

11.

Hurt Bert

I realized two things about myself the other day in Omaha, as I was shooting Jäger Bombs with a bunch of frat boys twenty years younger than I am. One: I don't like Jäger-meister. Two: I don't say no enough.

I'm like a ten-dollar hooker with a twelve-dollar-a-day habit. I rarely say no to anyone. It is one thing I consistently try to change about myself but never can. I'm sure my inability to say no is one of the main reasons I accrue crazy stories, and it is definitely the reason I am working in television today. Most of my comedian friends pick and choose their projects like prom queens picking shoes, and they will often tell you the most powerful word in this business is *no*. But I have always opted for the easy and comfortable *yes*.

"Yes, I'll slide down this snow-covered mountain at 60 mph with the legislative end of a shovel jutting between my legs. I'd love to. Just let me strap into this human slingshot first. Or better yet, why don't I be the first paying customer to jump off the tallest building west of the Mississippi? These all sound like great ideas I just can't say no to!"

I'm not going to tell you this is a rule for success—in entertainment or in life. In fact, I can look back and count dozens of times when I should have walked away. But this much is for sure: If I were the kind of guy who said "no" even once in his life, I would never have fought a bear.

Grappling with a bear was just one in a series of poor decisions I made when I said yes to filming a show called *Hurt Bert*. *Hurt Bert* had a simple premise. I would take dangerous jobs for one day with no training, insight, or preparation.

For the first shoot, I was an exterminator. All I knew about exterminators in Southern California was they sometimes ran up on rattlesnakes, and I wanted absolutely nothing to do with rattlesnakes. What I hadn't anticipated was that this job entailed wearing coveralls, a mask, and gloves (in the summer), and crawling under a house infested with rats. To hedge their bets, production made sure it was brimming with rats by hiring a handler who, I found out later, had crawled under the house thirty minutes before I did, and was literally setting rats on me. I was under the house for another thirty minutes while he made it rain rodents.

That was my initiation into reality television. What followed was a list of jobs that certain men are employed to do. Men with high blood pressure who don't qualify for life insurance: pro football players, pro hockey players, dominatrix gimps, stunt pilots, mixed martial arts (MMA) fighters, great-white-shark photographers, and lion tamers. Each show consisted of five to six segments and we needed to fill six shows.

My production team, in hopes of an Emmy nomination, would prod the best performances out of my cast mates. So for instance, when I was an MMA fighter, they set me against the First Family of Brazilian Ju-Jitsu, the Gracies. Instead of fighting one of them, though, I fought four. Production mentioned subtly in their pre-interview that I didn't care much for Brazilians, and that I'd said privately that they couldn't choke me out. If it wasn't fighters, they'd piss off the lions, antagonize the hockey players, or tell the stunt pilot to stall the plane long enough for me to grab my parachute and punch out.

One day we played Arena Football, and they set me up as the quarterback for the Los Angeles Avengers. Arena Football at that time had none of the trappings of Pro football—none of the infrastructure, none of the glam, and I'm sure none of the drug testing. These were hard-core dudes, some with very visible chips on their shoulders, who only knew how to play the game one way and that was head-first and hard. It was after practice one day that we joined them, and as we stepped onto the field I noticed the whole team watching me like it was my first day on the yard in prison. They were whistling, laughing, and pointing at me, as if they were figuring out the best way to have group sex with me. I assumed very quickly, and quite correctly, that the offensive line was not going to put up much of an effort in my defense. So, I took the first snap, took one step back, then ran up the middle through the defenders, into the end zone for a touchdown. As I ripped off my helmet and began an elaborate touchdown celebration, dancing as if I were at a powwow, I noticed the defensive coordinator throwing his hat on the ground and grabbing his linemen by their facemasks.

"This is why you're all third-string defensive linemen!" His face grew redder and his voice started sounding German as I heard my execution orders being shouted in their faces.

"This guy is a stand-up comedian and he just blew your doors off. You better redeem yourselves and put this man on a stretcher or I will kick you off this goddamn team today!"

As I got back in the huddle, my wide receiver smiled

at me. "I think we should do a passing play." He then looked around to the rest of the offense and said, "What do you guys think?"

They all smiled and nodded.

"So just drop back four steps, take your time, and see if you can hit me across the middle."

"How deep are you going?"

"I wouldn't worry yourself with the details," said a large offensive lineman, as he chuckled to the rest of the players in the huddle.

I dismissed them and we met back at the line, where I could hear phrases like, "We going fuck you up, Bert" mumbled through mouth guards. I called hike, took four steps back, and then everything went silent.

That is what a concussion sounds like.

I learned to distrust everyone I worked with. If I mentioned to a production assistant that I didn't like heights, he would run off and tell the producers. Next thing you know, I'm a roofer, only blindfolded, perched atop a three-story house.

After four episodes, two concussions, lacerations from an attack dog, two broken ribs, a bruised shin from a errant hockey puck, a broken foot, a bruised elbow, and a left leg that wouldn't stop shaking every time I yawned, I told them I thought it would work better if they simply told me what I was going to do so I could prepare some material or even some questions, rather than stand there like a crash-test dummy with a high-pitched squeal. So you can imagine my trepidation when, after taking my advice, they called and asked me, "Do you wanna fight a bear?"

"Who does that for a living?" I asked.

"You do, on Thursday."

A few things should be noted before we move forward. I was getting paid handsomely for this show, and I felt like we were breaking new ground in TV. I was spending time with some extremely interesting and unique men, men with amazing stories and intriguing insights. Add to that the fact that I was the star, had my name in the title, and despite having no actual involvement in production was billed as a "producer" on the show, you can understand why I might be willing to give anything they came up with a shot.

Having said that, it should also be noted that by the time they asked me to fight a bear, I had already learned I didn't enjoy working with large animals. Working with a large animal is like working with a porn star: you never know what kind of mood they are in, they don't know how to act, and the next day someone will definitely be shitting blood.

Prior to that call, I had already been mauled by a bull. With absolutely no training beyond how to put on clown makeup, which, oddly enough, freaked me out, I was put in the ring with a one-ton bull as a rodeo clown. The bull left me with two broken ribs, a broken foot, and only fifteen seconds of usable footage.

And that's the problem you run into working with animals. You can't reason with them the way you'd like.

"We already got the shot, so you don't need to break my ribs or my foot on the second take. Let's just go half speed for coverage."

Bull grunts his approval.

"Seriously, we get close, a few fly by shots at 40 percent will look 100 percent on TV. You'll look majestic, scary, proud. Your agent will be happy. You'll like the way this turns out, it'll look killer on your reel."

Bull grunts again.

"Alright, so let's get it on its feet!"

The bull and I fist-bump and make it explode as we walk into position.

One time I worked with a chimp and everyone howled with laughter as the chimp sat on my shoulders and grabbed both of my ears. I started playing up my fear, going all wide-eyed and squealy for the cameras, when I felt the genuine strength of the chimp lock onto me. It felt similar to when a child is on your shoulders and you lean back and feel their muscles tense in panic, only I wasn't leaning and this child had the strength of eight men. He wrapped an arm around my head and tightened his legs around my neck as if to suggest, "This head is mine if I want it." I stopped squealing and went Helen Keller silent, which made everyone on the set laugh even harder as they saw real fear enter my eyes, the kind of fear that has a scream and panic right behind it. The trainer came to the rescue and I jokingly mentioned to him that I had gotten scared for a second. Emotionless, the trainer said, "Yeah, I noticed him starting to freak."

"What would have happened?"

"Well, the first thing a chimp does is he bites off your fingers and genitals, then he goes for your face."

I laughed at his joke, thinking this guy had a wicked imagination. "Good thing that didn't happen?"

The trainer looked me dead in the eye, with no smile at all, and said, "Yeah, we were very lucky."

My call time to work with the bear was early in the morning. Apparently, just like meth addicts and homeless people, that's when bears like to fight. This far into the production schedule, however, I had accumulated a small hankering for Xanax, so mornings weren't my strong suit. Xanax rolls credits about an hour after you take one, and if you follow it with a couple of brewskies (which is a fun word to say when you're eating Xanax), the curtains don't draw back for your next show until matinee time. I got picked up—early—and roughly forty miles away from Los Angeles. During the whole car ride, I kept thinking that I wasn't so much getting closer to the shoot as I was farther and farther away from the best doctors.

As we pulled up to the location I was met by my field producer, Tim Scott, a cherubic man from Minnesota who dressed and acted like a character from *Fargo*. He was dry and had a wholesome look like a TV character from the 1950s, with a flattop to boot. He didn't look or act like someone in show business, and he was the kind of producer who boiled a dozen eggs for the crew the night before a shoot instead of getting craft services. Tim and I were friends, despite his job of putting me in eminent danger daily. He was a soldier following orders, and I completely understood that. It didn't help, however, when I saw him get excited about a segment, and today he was smiling from ear to ear.

"Do you think you're allergic to bears?"

I took a second to think about it, "Gee, Tim, I don't know. They don't really test for that at the allergist."

"I just think it would be funny if your face got all puffy and you couldn't breathe."

"Yeah, that would be a gas."

"You gotta see this thing," he said, bouncing next to me as we walked into the animal trainer's compound. "The bear you're gonna fight is huge!"

I couldn't exactly share in his excitement as I started to take in my surroundings. This was supposed to be a first-rate Hollywood-animal training facility, but it looked more like a zoo inside a crystal meth lab. As we walked, we passed an ark's worth of animals, ranging from a de-pressive elephant to an enraged tiger, finally approaching the bear. Tim explained the day's events.

"So the guy is gonna let you do everything: fight the

bear, tame lions, wash the elephant, and fuck around with the tiger if he can get him to calm down. It's gonna be awesome, but I thought we would start you slow and let you fight the baby of the bear, before the bear."

"Wrong," I said. "Everything I know about bears tells me not to fuck with their kids. How about I just fight the dad and we move on."

"Totally cool, I just thought it would make you more comfortable to work your way up."

As we turned the corner I saw the crew, a couple trainers, and a six-foot bear on a leash. Tim called to them. "He just wants to fight the dad. You can put that one back in the cage."

My heart sank as they walked the bear that was my height and only four times my weight off set. "That's not the dad?"

"No, that's the baby. There is the dad."

I looked where Tim was pointing and saw my opponent, a mound of what looked to be nine feet and roughly one thousand pounds of adult male bear, minding his own business, sitting casually on a park bench.

My first instinct was to walk right up to the bear and let him sniff my hand, to let him know I was a trusting kind of guy. But the trainer flipped the fuck out.

"You're breaking protocol!"

Tim pulled me aside and told me that, just like a rock star, there was a special way you had to meet the bear. The

trainer then came over and handed me five marshmallows.

"When the bear's not looking," he said, "take one of
the marshmallows and put it in your mouth, then casually
walk in front of the bear, show him the marshmallow, and
allow him the opportunity to engage with you and take
the marshmallow out of your mouth with his mouth. This
way he will learn to trust you."

I very politely nodded, smiled, then looked at both the
trainer and Tim. "Fuck that! Are you out of your fucking
mind? It's a nine-foot bear and you want me to make out
with him?"

"Yes," said the trainer. "Five times."

"Look," Tim said, pulling me aside, "he has been doing it all day and the bear is cool with it. You'll be fine,
trust me. Plus, the bear has to trust you if you want to
fight it."

"Tim, I want to trust the fucking bear before he trusts
me!"

"Trust needs to go both ways."

"What are you, a fucking minister? We are talking
about a bear, Tim."

"You'll be fine."

So, knowing no better, I took this man's word as truth
and grabbed the five marshmallows. I then casually
walked behind the bear, praying to God this would work.
I took a marshmallow and slipped it into my mouth.

Then, like a hooker, I casually walked in front of the bear, showing it to him. At first the bear didn't notice me, so, like any good ho, I buckled down and worked my corner. This worked—too well in my opinion—because the bear hopped to his feet quickly and in one fluid, semienthusiastic motion, slammed his face into my face and sucked the marshmallow out of my mouth. I assume we are all on the same page when it comes to a bear's oral hygiene: it's non-existent. Raw meat, bits of fur, plenty of saliva. Basically, I was making out with a homeless person, five times. And by the fifth time everyone was smiling, all for different reasons. The trainer was happy that the bear trusted me, my crew was happy their overpaid host just got tongue-kissed by a bear, and the bear was happy because he just met the marshmallow man. The trainer slapped me on the back, smiled to my crew, nodded to the bear, and proclaimed, "We're ready!"

Usually any type of approval makes me bubble, but with this I had a bit of hesitation. "Hold on, I haven't learned anything."

He smiled. "My friend, you've learned the most important thing you need to know about this bear, and that is, he loves marshmallows. So if you feel like you're in trouble, very confidently say 'marshmallow.' Two things will happen. Number one, the bear will think you're getting him another marshmallow. More importantly, we'll know you are in trouble and we'll get you out of there."

He took a pause, looked over my shoulder, smiled, and said, "Alright, he's ready. Let's go."

Sounded super simple. The bear was a creature of habit, just like me. For him it was marshmallows, for me it was the case of beer waiting in the cooler. There is no better feeling than finishing a day of work and cracking a cold one with a crew, who can finally take the gear off their shoulders and rest. The bear had the same ritual. Do your job, get a marshmallow, a pat on the forehead, and a slow walk to the cage. I found a moment of solidarity with the bear. We were compadres, coworkers, doing a job for our handlers, a job they couldn't do.

I turned and immediately our connection disappeared. The bear was on top of me. He grabbed me by both ears and clutched tightly onto my head with his paws. I felt his claws—not even neatly trimmed, I might add—secure a grip on my head as I began to shout.

"*Marshmallow.*"

I could barely hear the words come out of my own mouth, mostly because his paws pressing tightly against my ears made everything silent. Also because my world became quieter with each and every one of his roars. He swung me back and forth several times before he slammed me directly into the center of his chest, practically motor-boating me into submission. To this day I have never felt more helpless than I did that day, gasping for air, sucking in bear fur, shouting "Marshmallow" into a bear's chest. I thought I was going to pass out, when all of a sudden everything spun bright. The bear had accidentally, or maybe purposely, let go of my head with one paw, holding it steady to his chest with the other, when he got a claw stuck in one of my belt loops, and with absolute hilarity spun me into a bear hug, doggy style.

Now facing the crew and appreciating fresh air, I took a deep breath and very calmly said, "Marshmallow." The crew broke out laughing, as the bear bent me over and held on tight.

Realizing I was killing, and feeling safe in comedy, I started hamming it up just a bit, with marshmallow as my punch line. I scanned my audience to see what part of the crowd I needed to focus on when I saw the look on the trainer's face. While Tim and the others were howling silently, as a crew will do when they love what they're shooting, the trainer was desperately trying to make eye contact with me. I saw the moment of discreet eye contact pass, and now he was shouting, "Go limp!"

Again, time slowed down, and I grew oddly introspective. I thought to myself, "Why is this the first I've heard of the 'go limp' thing? We've never gone over this. How limp am I supposed to go? A little-soft limp, drunk limp, look-unattractive-to-a-fat-chick-you-had-sex-with-in-college-and-now-she-wants-to-see-if-it's-cool-if-she-spends-the-night limp? Or just play-it-by-ear limp? Come to think of it, I hope he's talking to me, and not telling the bear to become unaroused. Is there bear cock climbing up my jeans, about to split the center seam?"

I quickly checked between my legs to make sure the trainer was talking to me—that the bear wasn't DTF—and after that was confirmed, I went Xanax limp. I slid out of the bear's grip and landed on my back. That's the last thing I remember. Apparently, as I lay on my back at the feet of the bear, he "instinctually" sat on my face. This is what they told me when I came to in Tim's lap under a tree and whimpered, "What happened?"

Tim smiled a big Midwestern smile and said, "You got raped and teabagged by a bear—and it was *hilarious*. Let's go tame lions!"

I went on to tame lions that day, wash an elephant, and stayed the fuck away from the tiger. The show got canceled before the bear segment ever aired. The network wanted more story arc and fewer short, non sequitur (but hilarious) clips. Their feeling was that people wanted story, so we went back to them with a new version of the same idea, wherein I would take the most dangerous job in the world for an entire season: I would be a crab fisherman on a boat in the Bering Strait for one fishing season while a camera crew followed me. The network passed. No one, they said, wanted to see a bunch of uneducated guys fish on a crab boat.

As I sit here today, I guess I could be bitter that the show wasn't a smash hit like Mike Rowe's *Dirty Jobs,* or that YouTube wasn't around yet to help promote a show that, in hindsight, was basically making viral videos, and which might have made me famous then (or at least Internet famous). Or I could even be upset that we didn't get the green light to make the *Deadliest Catch*, three years before the *Deadliest Catch* premiered.

Instead I sit here today grateful that my legacy wasn't cemented that day. Imagine it: Bert Kreischer. On-air talent. Comedian. Got fucked in the ass to death by a bear on camera.

12.

The Importance of Being Soft

I'm not a really deep dude. I like beer, cheeseburgers, and blow jobs. I love parties, especially when they start in the afternoon, and as far as feelings go, I'm always up for the good ones and live with a constant fear of the bad ones. I sleep with my mouth open, I watch porn, I'll smoke pot if it's passed to me, and I love a good dick joke. I've been in love a couple of times and had my heart broken almost exactly the same number of times. I don't speak to any of those women, they are dead to me. That's how I operate. I'm fine with most artistic criticism and professional failure. I find that if criticism comes from a respectable source and ultimately facilitates more blow jobs, beers, and burgers, I can work through it. And as far as failure, it just comes with the territory of the business I'm in.

As a husband I'm okay. I kind of remember birthdays and try to talk, touch, and listen five minutes before sex, as I am told that is what women want and the best way to get what I want. I'm probably worse as a dad. To be honest, I had no idea that having kids was going to involve so much commitment. I thought it was going to be making a grilled cheese here, driving a road trip there, a kiss on the forehead, a tuck in at night, maybe a spanking, and we're done. The idea that my kids would become my entire life, everything I work for and toward, and that their successes and failures would define my happiness, and that I would never have the heart to hit them, was well beyond me when I got my wife pregnant.

I remember the first night with my first daughter, Georgia. She cried and cried and cried, and I felt completely and totally helpless, praying, as I lay on a cot at the foot of my wife LeeAnn's hospital bed, that my mom would miraculously appear and "take care of this noise."

Slowly I realized, this is going to be me. Me, for the next thirty years plus, taking care of this child, raising her, grooming her for life so she didn't have to cry and would be happy. But how do I make her happy? Panic struck through my heart as the nurse came in and told me exactly how. Hold her head by my heart, place my pinky finger on her bottom lip, and allow her to draw it in to "suckle," which she did. She sucked on my finger like she was trying to rip my nail off, and she immediately relaxed. Panic struck again: Is this how you groom a whore?

"We are stopping this *tonight*. I'm not raising a daughter who chugs cock to calm down every time she gets freaked out!" I wanted better for my little girl.

Then the second daughter came and I had the same moment in the same hospital, my newborn crying her first evening cry. I tried to take in the beauty of the moment: my gorgeous wife, our healthy daughters, Georgia and Ila, the fact that this time around I wasn't scared of the unknown. Instead all I could think to myself was, "Why the fuck did I do this again?" It must be how you feel when you wake up hungover with a brand-new face tattoo. I couldn't wait to look at it, but the idea of living with it was overwhelming.

I love my girls. I also love whiskey, and I come by both loves honestly. Jameson is my family's whiskey. If you're Irish, you're faithful to one of two Irish whiskeys: Jameson or Bushmills. My family has always been a Jameson family. If there were ever any doubt about my allegiance to it, it ended in 2007 when as a father of a one-year-old and a three-year-old, the Lord kissed me on the forehead and I became sponsored by Jameson to go on the road with five other comics on a national tour.

It was amazing, especially for a group that my buddy and fellow comedian Billy Gardell called a "bunch of

$900-a-week road comics." Every week, four of us would fly first class to a different city, get picked up in town cars, driven to five-star hotels, do twenty minutes of stand-up each, and get paid eight times what we were worth. Our only rule was we had to drink Jameson before, during, and after the show. Oh, and once a year they would fly us to Ireland to hang out at the distillery, do a show, and do radio. Talk about being thrown into the briar patch. I was literally living in a dream. We comics were not only having a blast, but we were growing closer and closer every week. It was me, Steve Byrne, Danny Bevins, Michael Loftus, Pete Correale, and Billy Gardell.

Billy was the leader of our pack for many reasons. He was the largest, the oldest, and the strongest comedian, but mostly, he had been doing this the longest and had more wisdom to offer than the rest. Michael Loftus was a TV writer who was trying to get back into stand-up. He was the smallest guy of the group and always walked on his tippy toes. Most people will say size doesn't matter, but in this group it was noticed, by us and by him. Loftus was easily the smartest of the group and the guy we all realized we'd be asking for a job from one day. Pete Correale smoked pot not just daily but hourly. He loved to laugh, loved to drink, and loved smoking cigarettes. He was a true comic in the cosmic sense—if you sent him in a time machine anywhere, anytime throughout history, he would have someone laughing, probably at some bar.

Danny Bevins had rage circling inside him like a school of sharks. He was ex-military and when he started drinking, the fins of his rage started peeking out above the surface. Those fins made a beeline for Loftus, who was waiting on his tippy-toes for them, ready to start punching shark noses. Steve Byrne was half Asian and my oldest friend of the group. We had both come out of New York. We were the same age and had the same manager, the same sense of humor, and the same interests. He hated Loftus.

I, on the other hand, was just over the moon about getting free Jameson. I was always loud and never listened to anyone much. A few of us had kids, all of us had drinking problems, and each of us found himself in a similar boat: married to women who understood what kind of man could leave his family for a weekend and miss them genuinely, but who would miss the road just as much when they were home.

The first weekend I met Billy was in Cincinnati. Billy generally closed the show, but when he wasn't there I did. Closing is a weird strength. It's the one spot out of the night that has to deal with the waitresses handing the patrons their checks, which more often than not they do quite loudly and with no concern for you or your attempts at comedy. To say that the check spot is a difficult one is an understatement. It's like being the last guy in a gang bang, charged with making sure the woman has had an orgasm.

But to have the check spot after three headlining, success-hungry, Jameson-filled comics who are absolute killers on stage, doing their tightest twenty minutes, is a losing proposition. It calls for a skill set not every comic has. You have to be aware enough to notice that the room is changing. You have to be able to find the people that are listening and connect with them. You have to have thick enough skin not to let the fact get to you that 80 percent of the room isn't listening. And you have to have enough material to roll with every- and anything that happens in that moment. You have to recognize when the room is done, and be able to pull out of that moment seamlessly, unfazed, and with enough respect for the crowd to close out hard and strong. All skills that are hardened with time and alcohol. It has nothing to do with being the funniest comic out there. But if you're the guy willing to take that bullet, then you are the funniest of the lot for at least that one night.

It was in Cincinnati that Billy conceded the role of funniest comic to me.

"I'm not following you and your Yosemite Sam shit!" he said when we first met. He was referring to the fact that I basically had no rules when it came to doing stand-up. Shirt off, people on stage, group shots, calling my wife, answering my phone, all stuff that makes a live performance all that more live and makes a more act-based comic extremely frustrated. I would veer toward chaos at any chance possible. Billy did not.

I looked at this behemoth of a man. "But you close the shows."

"Not tonight I don't, I'm going third and you're closing."

I shared my concerns, my ego inflating a bit as Billy told me, in no uncertain terms, that he didn't want to follow me.

"Look, you're young, hungry, funny, and you want this shit. I'm an old man just looking for a paycheck. I'll tell my little jokes, ease up a bit before I get off, pump the brakes, and then bring you up real nice."

Done! I thought. What a massive compliment, to be asked to follow a hard-core road killer doing his tightest twenty.

We had already done the business of figuring out the lineup. That was over. Now to the best part of being a comic. We sat in the greenroom for the next hour before Billy went up, gossiping about all things comics love to gossip about: who was funny, who stole, which comics hated each other, who we liked, who we couldn't stand, where we started, who we started with, what our goals were. As long as I live I will never connect quicker or easier with anyone in the world than I do with other comedians. There's a shorthand that can't be understood by noncomics. You don't get it from doing a couple open mics, and you don't even get it by hanging around comedians. You have to earn it. And once you've earned it, you look for those like you who have earned it, too.

That night in Cincinnati, we sat in that greenroom with the door shut, drinking whiskey and talking, until the sound guy knocked to tell Billy he had just given Loftus the light, warning him that his twenty-minute set was almost up. Billy got up, just like an old factory worker getting off of the break bench. He put out his cigarette and punched in for the evening.

Billy proceeded to *destroy* the crowd with what I still consider the tightest twenty-minute set I have ever seen. When the sound guy gave him the light, I went back to the bar and grabbed a fresh Jameson, hastily returning to see exactly how Billy was going to slow down the insane momentum he had built with the crowd. I saw that his "pumping the brakes" wasn't working out exactly like he had planned. It was more like he was spinning wildly down the mountain, giggling as the car careened out of control. I took a big swig of Jameson, listened to him call my name, and like most comics do in moments of fear, went in and went through the motions.

My set went well—well enough not to slow down the show's momentum much. The crowd gave us a standing ovation as the four of us stood on stage for a mini curtain call. We went out that night and drank hard. We talked shit, boosted each other's egos, and generally hit it off before stumbling back to our rooms, leaving Loftus and Danny to argue about the war in Iraq.

The next night's early set unfolded exactly like the previous, only this time, Billy seemed to be pumping the gas a lot harder as his set wrapped up. I did my best to carry the momentum. I found myself with no choice but to bring a waitress onstage and have her sing while I did a strip tease. This pleased the crowd to no end—even the other comics enjoyed it. I stood almost naked onstage, with nothing but a boot covering my junk. At the end of her song, the other three guys rushed the stage, shots in hand. I was beside myself with joy. My work on stage was so moving that my peers felt the need to join me. No bigger compliment can be paid to a comic than to have the comics he respects watch him from the back of the room and want to share the spotlight with him. Billy grabbed the mic and proclaimed to the crowd, "We are the Jameson Comedy Tour and this wild man is our headliner, Bert Kreischer. Thank you guys for coming out." We took our shot and he wrapped his big arm around me. He pulled me in close and whispered, "You got ten more minutes, asshole."

My excitement turned to panic as they left me on stage and I tried to calmly and confidently redress, the crowd watching open-mouthed for me to top what just happened. I had mistimed the closing of the show, and Billy and the guys knew that. Now I felt like a fat stripper. Rather than sit silently by and watch me fail, they took pleasure in joining in, putting a sort of cruel icing on the cake. They knew that after that, I would have nothing but stale material to offer the crowd.

Backstage, before our second set of the night began, we laughed as we recounted my miscalculation. That's when my phone rang. It was my wife. I was dying to tell her just how funny the moment was, and I quickly picked up.

"Hey babe, you're never gonna believe what just happened."

My enthusiasm was met with seriousness.

"I need to talk to you. Are you alone?"

"No, I'm with the guys. What's up?"

"We've had an accident and Georgia's been hurt."

My heart sank, as did my face. The guys noticed and stopped laughing.

Women are amazing animals when it comes to drama. She had called ten months earlier while I was in Houston and I answered the phone to hysterical crying. Panic raced through me as I tried to decipher what she was sobbing out on the other line. Our kids were dead? She had been assaulted? My dad was dead? My sisters?

No, it was her fucking cat.

Click.

I hung up angry that she couldn't have gone into the bedroom, pulled her shit together for a minute, and called and told me the news, rather than letting me guess like some scene in a horror movie.

This time she was cold and calculated, and that's what scared me.

She went on to tell me the details: Georgia, our three-year-old, had been walking into our apartment lobby and had tripped in her Crocs. She fell face-first on the marble floor, landing on her top jaw, breaking it and her four front teeth, under the gum line. LeeAnn told me they had been to the hospital and had scheduled an appointment with an oral surgeon in Beverly Hills for the day after next. The last thing she told me, which she needn't have, was that I was to get back to California immediately.

I hung up the phone and looked at my three friends.

"I have to go home."

I relayed the events to them and, most of them having children, they sincerely empathized. That is when the club manager Rick walked through the doors of the greenroom. "I'm starting the music, you guys ready?"

Danny pulled him out of the room and told him the news as Billy and Mike rolled a zone defense on my mini-downward spiral. Danny came back in with four Jamesons on the rocks.

"I talked to Rick and told him what was going on. He gave me these. I'm no doctor but I do know that these usually make things better in the short term."

We all grabbed a Jameson. Billy stood up and put his

hand on my shoulder and said, "Listen, your old lady said she is doing okay now. We'll get you home in the morning, everything is gonna be fine. It could have been a helluva lot worse. Pull it together. We'll all deal with this shit after the show, like brothers. But you're still going last."

The room laughed, as did I, and we did our shots. It was almost nice to know that there was no pressure following Billy this time. I knew I had to go onstage—I wasn't going to go back to my hotel and stew in my thoughts. I called LeeAnn one more time after the show started and did some more investigation. LeeAnn was a lot lighter. Georgia seemed fine, she was playing in her room. The doctor had told LeeAnn not to make a big deal out of it. The schedule was firm, though, and they needed to get Georgia into surgery ASAP to make sure an infection wasn't setting in. I guess so, anyway. I don't know for sure since I was barely listening. Because what I had heard was they'd need to put her under, which could be tricky. I made plans to return on the first flight out the next morning.

I'd love to tell you that I pulled out one of my all-time best sets of comedy that night, while under duress. But I can't. I went through the motions, and I don't remember anything but the walk home. We were all meandering slowly, me and the other comics, respecting the gravity of the situation—not barhopping ourselves home as usual, Loftus and Danny getting along—when Billy again wrapped his arm around me.

"I'm not gonna tell you your business, you're a grown man, but I think the worst thing you can do right now is run to a bottle."

I nodded slowly.

"Having said that, you say the word and we will all sit with you and drink until your flight tomorrow morning."

I chose the latter. We stayed up and drank Jameson until I was drunk enough to cry. They left me in my room to pack and shower. Before I took off in the early morning, Billy called to see if I wanted one more, which I did. I got it to go, hopped in my cab, and cried the entire way to the airport. My inhibitions were gone and my emotions ran free. Fear and anger were the most prevalent. I felt like I had been tricked into all these emotions I couldn't control. For Christ's sake, when I first met my wife, I had just wanted to fuck her, that was all. All I could think now was that I hadn't signed up for this. I was cool with marriage and I was cool with kids. I sincerely loved having both. But these feelings of vulnerability—I was not cool with this.

I was angry with my wife. When we met, she said she had no intentions of changing who I was. The comedy, the drinking, the partying she was all cool with, and I believed her. But that had all been part of her diabolical plan. The guy she met back then, the old Bert, would have never sobbed uncontrollably in the back of a taxi for thirty minutes. The guy she met didn't cry at all. But she knew, without a doubt, that the second she introduced kids into the picture I would inevitably, without my consent or knowledge, become a different man. It was like a heroin dealer who tells a new customer, "There are *a lot* of people who use it recreationally. The rumors about heroin's addictive qualities are highly exaggerated."

I cleaned myself up as we pulled up to the airport, watching the cabbie try to decipher the events that led to this awkward 4 A.M. cab ride to the airport. I imagine he thought I must have been some scorned gay lover, who had spent the night tied and bound while the love of my life, who I had flown out here to see, had his way with me, not even letting me climax, only to be told at 3:30 A.M. that I was just one of his many fuck buddies and that my plan to stay with him while he was at a conference in Cincinnati was in no way feasible, as he had his wife and kids coming in today. And to think that I had bought us tickets to the Reds game months in advance to watch that kid with the big arm pitch. But now I was on my way, heart broken, balls blue, to the airport.

That is definitely what he must have been thinking as I paid him with tear-soaked bills. But I didn't care. I downed my roadie and made my way to the plane.

I held it together pretty well until takeoff when the anxiety of the flight, the booze in my system, and my goddamn bitch-ass vulnerability kicked in. The flight attendant approached me—my sunglasses on, covered in my hoodie—

and inquired. I told her my daughter was hurt and that I was flying home to see her. She came back with a whiskey and asked no more questions. The next time she walked past me she handed me another.

By the time I hopped in a cab at LAX, the crying had stopped. I was making my way back to Hollywood when my phone rang. It was LeeAnn.

"Listen, when you get here, have your shit together. No crying, no dramatics."

"Not a problem," I promised her, as I motioned for the cab driver to pull over at a 7-Eleven. I hopped out, grabbed a forty and a coffee, and downed them in that order. I was set to be the dad I'd always envisioned. Probably the first time on record I had ever stepped up to be a great dad, needless to say, but I was ready.

I walked in the house like a soldier. I empathized, I played, I read books, we watched a movie, and Georgia eventually went to sleep.

That night LeeAnn broke it down for me. "I want you to eat a Xanax tomorrow before we head to the dentist. It's going to be pretty stressful and I need you to be calm."

Usually being told to take drugs means a good time for me, but this time it raised concern. "How stressful?"

"Putting a child under is not easy and can be dicey. They told me today the most important thing for us to do is keep her calm. They said if she's calm, everything would be fine. So I can't have you joking around, touching things, distracting people because you're nervous. So I think you should take a Xanax and just relax. It's all gonna be fine."

That was all I needed to hear. I'd lube up early in the morning like a rock star heading to press, we'd roll in, they'd put her under, pull the teeth, set the jaw, and I'd be celebrating with a glass of Jameson that night, slow-rolling that early morning buzz. Done.

Our appointment was for 7 A.M. and I had been drinking fairly heavily for three days straight. LeeAnn woke us all up at 6:30 and we made our way to the car. I popped a Xanax on Wilshire, halfway to Beverly Hills, and felt the tranquility set in. I was even more relaxed when I saw that LeeAnn, always very budget minded, decided in a moment of emergency to do the right thing and get Georgia a high-priced Beverly Hills oral surgeon with a shingle on Rodeo Drive. Had it been for herself, LeeAnn would have booked a hack in a strip mall on San Vicente. But she knew what was important.

When we walked into the empty waiting room, it was clear they were here for us. None of the formalities of signing paperwork, no waiting—they took us directly back to the chair like I was Hugh Hefner at Planned Parenthood. The surgeon and anesthesiologist introduced themselves and assured us that everything was going to be fine. My Xanax hadn't fully kicked in but things were moving so smoothly that I felt silly for even taking it. The surgeon and anesthesiologist even went so far as to brag to us about how great the other was, basically sucking each other's cocks for our benefit, which I appreciated.

I was all smiles until they went to put Georgia under. That's when hell broke loose.

Georgia didn't want to be in the chair by herself. This was a deal breaker in her eyes. Kids can be real douche bags about getting their way, and in this moment, Georgia was no exception. Her demands were that Mommy and Daddy be in the chair with her. I remember when I was a kid getting stitches above my eye and saying the same thing. My mom held firm, said no, and then strapped me to a backboard like a lunatic getting an emergency circumcision. We held a hard line, then drew her attention to the other side of the chair, as we motioned for the anesthesiologist to do his dirty work with the needle. But to our dismay, this overpriced fuckface "couldn't find a vein," which is a gentler way of saying that he stabbed my daughter in the arm with a needle ten times as she wailed and writhed uncontrollably. I could see that we were failing in our mandate to "keep her calm." That's when the anesthesiologist pulled me aside.

"I'm gonna need you to put her under."

My jaw almost broke, too, as it hit the floor.

"I spent seven years in college. I cheated on my driver's license exam. I'm not sure I'm the guy for the job."

"Listen," he said intensely, "we need to give her the

gas, and I need her breathing evenly. This is very important. It's better if you do it. She trusts you."

"And I trusted that you would be able to do your job,
yet here we are."

"You are her father and you need to do this now."

I looked to LeeAnn and I could see that for the first
time since Georgia fell two days ago, she was starting to
fall apart. She had been the mother every person dreams
of and the wife you could only imagine, but the sight of her
daughter screaming in pain, scared and alone on a chair,
was too much for her. This is a woman who raised herself
and has never shown me she was scared, yet there she was,
standing like I had, the day she gave birth, south of the
gurney, when I learned what an episiotomy was.

So I manned the fuck up.

I walked over to the chair and knelt beside Georgia.
"Hey, baby, here is the deal. We're not gonna do the needle
anymore."

"Thanks, Daddy."

"I told that guy no more needle, not on my little girl!"

"Thanks, Daddy, they really hurt."

"Yeah, I had no idea he was going to do that, he's a
real jerk and I'm gonna put him in a time-out after this."

She leaned up to hug me as I watched the rest of the
room collectively roll their eyes—all but the anesthesiologist, who eyed me to hurry things up.

"Here's the deal. I got this sweet-smelling gas. You

just got to sniff it and you'll go to sleep. Then they can fix your teeth, and, *bam*, we go home and get ice cream!"

"I'll go to sleep?"

"Yup, just like that and then we get ice cream!"

"What if I don't wake up?"

My heart sank. I realized that was the question that had been haunting me this whole time. What if she didn't wake up? How was I supposed to deal with that? How was I ever going to know joy again? My life would be fucked. Surely I would never be able to find humor in anything ever again, so what would I do for a living? Work at Home Depot? And from a practical standpoint, what would we do with her body? Would we take it home with us? I definitely couldn't leave it in Beverly Hills with a bunch of strangers who I'm sure would just put it in a closet until the coroner came to get it. I'd need it with me. Would they let me take it home or would I have to sneak it out casually? And how would I sneak her body out of a dentist's office—down an elevator and casually wait at valet with it as they brought my car around?

As all these thoughts flooded my head, I looked my daughter in the eyes.

"Good question. Let me ask."

I walked over to the doctors. "What if she doesn't wake up?"

The anesthesiologist said, "Listen, Dad, you need to do this now."

I may have my shortcomings as a father and as a human being, but if nothing else, I take direction well.

I did an about-face, walked directly to her chair, grabbed the mask, whispered, "I love you, this is gonna be fine," and then smothered my daughter like Lenny from *Of Mice and Men*. She fought me for a couple of seconds, but my 220-pound frame was more than she could handle. I could hear the dentist jokingly say to the anesthesiologist, "That's one way to do it," as her body went limp. They pulled me off her and went to work. I looked over and saw LeeAnn crying. In my head all I could hear was a voice whispering, "She is crying because she watched you kill your daughter."

And that is when the floodgates reopened. I began crying a "first night in prison" cry, which seemed to be acceptable, until it escalated into a "first rape in prison" cry. The nurses escorted me out of the room, for fear that my crying might wake up my daughter, and into a bathroom. There it only got worse. It seemed so silly to me, the idea of facing myself in a bathroom mirror and crying, that I began laughing while I was crying, which must have sounded from the outside like someone was stabbing a clown. The idea of laughing at this moment pissed me off, but I couldn't help it. Watching myself cry in a mirror looked hilarious. I looked so absolutely foolish. It was as if the old, childless Bert was looking at the new Bert and laughing back at him. I could hear him saying to me, "I told you, bitch. You're weak, son!"

But the fact was that childless Bert was history. There was only me now, a man who loved his family so dearly that he gassed his own daughter, possibly killing her in the process.

I left the bathroom, and the man laughing back at me in the mirror, and walked into the waiting room. Apparently in the time it took us to get her under, the office had opened for business. As I took a seat next to LeeAnn— still in tears, both of us—I saw a boy to our left tug on his dad's coat sleeve, and whisper something to him. I'm sure it was about my crying. Something to the effect of, "I thought you said this wasn't going to be that bad."

Directly across from us was a black woman who I could tell desperately wanted to make eye contact. For a second I entertained the thought; after all, black women have an innate soothing sense in times of need (see *The Matrix*). But my eyes were too filled with tears to make eye contact with anyone. The room was a blurred mess.

This is when the Xanax really kicked in.

The good and bad about Xanax is that it makes you very comfortable in not-so-comfortable situations, which could mean that, say you were crying in front of a bunch of strangers, your discomfort might subside, and suddenly you look and feel absolutely fine. Or, it could take away the shame you felt about your crying, and the discomfort that you were putting others through, and allow you to just let the waterfall flow. That's what happened to me. I've done a lot of awkward things on Xanax—bragging at Thanksgiving dinner about a blow job I had gotten, holding a stranger's hand in turbulence and realizing only afterward that he was not cool with it. That day I cried like no one has ever seen a man cry. Openly, honestly, and fearlessly for ten fucking minutes. I sobbed out phrases like, "I'm a daddy," "I love her," and "We need to take her home, I want her body" so intensely that when the door opened and the dentist came out and discreetly said to us, "She is okay. You can come back and get her," the room broke into applause. We walked the few short steps from the waiting room. Georgia was still sound asleep in her room, bloody gauze hanging out her mouth.

"She did great," they said, which I found to be a bit insulting considering I did all the hard work. She had done nothing but lie there unconscious. But I didn't argue. Lee-Ann picked her up and they sent us to a recovery room to let her wake up naturally.

In the recovery room I realized exactly how expensive this dentist was going to be. They had a leather couch, candles, and music playing in the background. I slid the curtain to close off our corner of the room and exhaled. I looked at LeeAnn and I saw her like I had never seen her before. It was a different version of the woman I met, a different version of sexy. This wasn't just a guy checking out a chick, but a man looking at a woman and all the traits she possessed, in awe. How had I been so lucky? I stared at her in silence, hoping in some alternate universe, by way of some small miracle, she saw in me what I was seeing in her.

That's when I heard the curtain open and saw the shock on LeeAnn's face. It was the black woman from the waiting room.

Whitney fucking Houston.

She gave me a hug and whispered, "It's hard being a daddy." She then sat on the couch with LeeAnn and Georgia, stroking Georgia's hair, and talked to us both about parenthood—the spoils that are promised and the heartache it came with. She sat with us for about ten minutes and we said nothing. She looked absolutely stunning as she filled the room with her words of wisdom, none of which I can remember—I was too busy hoping she would start singing to my daughter. (She didn't.) She gracefully left, wished us luck, and we sat in silence as she closed the curtain behind her.

LeeAnn mouthed to me, *"Whitney fucking Houston."*

We took Georgia home, put her in bed, and took naps ourselves. That night LeeAnn told me the tooth fairy needed to get himself to the toy store and get some gifts. This was a big deal and, in this situation, a quarter just would not do.

I went to the store, and as I walked up and down the toy section, I felt a pride I had never felt before. I had been through the thick of a difficult situation and made it to the other side. I had two healthy, happy children despite one being almost toothless, and a woman who was the best partner since Clyde met Bonnie. I could provide for my family on the road, but also step up and be a man and a father when the situation demanded it. I had cried in front of strangers but was cool with it. I was vulnerable, and I was cool with that, too. I was a dad, first and foremost, and no amount of partying, drinking, or touring would ever change that.

But there was one takeaway that was more important than the rest, and that was this: I met Whitney Houston. And that would have never happened if I hadn't become a dad.